Facts and Fallacies
of Software Engineering

Facts and Fallacies
of Software Engineering

Robert L. Glass

✦✦ Addison-Wesley

Boston • San Francisco • New York • Toronto • Montreal
London • Munich • Paris • Madrid
Capetown • Sydney • Tokyo • Singapore • Mexico City

The publisher offers discounts on this book when ordered in quantity for bulk purchases and special sales. For more information, please contact:

U.S. Corporate and Government Sales
(800) 382-3419
corpsales@pearsontechgroup.com

For sales outside of the United States, please contact:

International Sales
(317) 581-3793
international@pearsontechgroup.com

Visit Addison-Wesley on the Web: *www.awprofessional.com*

Library of Congress Cataloging-in-Publication Data

Glass, Robert L., 1932–
    Facts and fallacies of software engineering / Robert L. Glass.
        p.   cm.
Includes bibliographical references and index.
ISBN 0-321-11742-5 (alk. paper)
  1. Software engineering   I. Title.

QA76.758 .G52 2003
005.1'068'5--dc21   2002027737

Text printed on recycled and acid-free paper.

ISBN 0321117425

4 5 6 7 8 9 PH   07 06 05 04

4th Printing   October 2004

This book is dedicated to the researchers
who lit the fire of software engineering and
to the practitioners who keep it burning.

Contents

Acknowledgments

To Paul Becker,
now of Addison-Wesley, who has been the editor for nearly all of my non-self-published books, for his belief in me over the years.

To Karl Wiegers,
for his contributions of frequently forgotten fundamental facts and for the massive job of reviewing and massaging what I wrote.

To James Bach, Vic Basili, Dave Card, Al Davis, Tom DeMarco, Yaacov Fenster, Shari Lawrence Pfleeger, Dennis Taylor, and Scott Woodfield,
for the hugely important task of helping me identify appropriate citations for the sources of these facts.

Foreword

When I first heard that Bob Glass was going to write this book and model it after my *201 Principles of Software Development*, I was a bit worried. After all, Bob is one of the best writers in the industry, and he would provide tough competition for my book. And then, when Bob asked me to write his foreword, I became even more worried; after all, how can I endorse a book that seems to compete directly with one of mine? Now that I have read *Facts and Fallacies of Software Engineering*, I am pleased and honored (and no longer worried!) to have the opportunity to write this foreword.

The software industry is in the same state of affairs that the pharmaceutical industry was in during the late nineteenth century. Sometimes it seems that we have more snake-oil salespeople and doomsayers than sensible folks practicing and preaching in our midst. Every day, we hear from somebody that they have discovered this great new cure for some insurmountable problem. Thus we have oft heard of quick cures for low efficiency, low quality, unhappy customers, poor communication, changing requirements, ineffective testing, poor management, and on and on. There are so many such pundits of the perfunctory that we sometimes wonder if perhaps some portion of the proclaimed panaceas are possibly practical. Whom do we ask? Whom in this industry can we trust? Where can we get the truth? The answer is Bob Glass.

Bob has had a history of providing us with short treatises on the many software disasters that have occurred over the years. I have been waiting for him to distill the common elements from these disasters so that we can benefit more easily from his many experiences. The 55 facts that Bob Glass discusses in this wonderful book are not just conjectures on his part. They are exactly what I have been waiting for: the wisdom gained by the author by examining in detail the hundreds of cases he has written about in the past.

The 55 facts that follow are likely not to be popular with all readers. Some are in direct opposition to the so-called modern ways of doing things. For those of you who wish to ignore the advice contained within these covers, I can wish you only the safest of journeys, but I fear for your safety. You are treading on well-trod territory, known to be full of mines, and many have destroyed their careers trying to pass. The best advice I can give you is to read any of Bob Glass's earlier books concerning software disasters. For those of you who wish to follow the advice contained herein, you too are following a well-trod path. However, this path is full of successful testimonies. It is a path of awareness and knowledge. Trust Bob Glass because he has been there before. He has had the privilege of analyzing his own successes and failures along with hundreds of others' successes and failures. Stand on his shoulders, and you will more likely succeed in this industry. Ignore his advice, and be prepared for Bob to call you in a few years to ask you about your project—to add it to his next compilation of software disaster stories.

Alan M. Davis
Spring 2002

Author's Addendum:
I tried to get Al Davis to tone down this foreword. It is, after all, a bit syrupy sweet. But he resisted all of my efforts. (I really *did* try! Honest!) In fact, in one such exchange, he said, "You deserve to be on a pedestal, and I'm happy to help you up!" My experience with being on pedestals is that, inevitably, you fall off, and when you do, you break into Humpty-Dumpty-like insignificant fragments.

But regardless of all that, I cannot imagine greater and more wonderful sentiments than the ones Al bestows on me here. Thanks!

Robert L. Glass
Summer 2002

PART 1

55 FACTS

Introduction

This book is a collection of facts and fallacies about the subject of software engineering.

Sounds boring, doesn't it? A laundry list of facts and fallacies about building software doesn't sound like the kind of thing you'd like to kick back and spend an hour or two with. But there's something special about these facts and fallacies. They're fundamental. And the truth that underlies them is frequently forgotten. In fact, that's the underlying theme of this book. A lot of what we ought to know about building software we don't, for one reason or another. And some of what we think we know is just plain wrong.

Who is the *we* in that previous paragraph? People who build software, of course. We seem to need to learn the same lessons over and over again, lessons that these facts—if remembered—might help us avoid. But by *we* I also mean people who do research about software. Some researchers get mired so deeply in theory that they miss some fundamentally important facts that might turn their theories upside-down.

So the audience for this book is anyone who's interested in building software. Professionals, both technologists and their managers. Students. Faculty. Researchers. I think, he said immodestly, that there's something in this book for all of you.

Originally, this book had a cumbersome, 13-word title: Fifty-Five Frequently Forgotten Fundamental Facts (and a Few Fallacies) about Software Engineering was, well, excessive—or at least those responsible for marketing this book thought so. So cooler heads prevailed. My publisher and I finally settled on Facts and Fallacies of Software Engineering. Crisp, clear—and considerably less colorful!

I had tried to shorten the original long title by nicknaming it the F-Book, noting the alliteration of all the letter *F*s in the title. But my publisher objected, and I suppose I have to admit he was right. After all, the letter F is probably the only dirty letter in our alphabet (*H* and *D* have their advocates, also, but *F* seems to reach another level of dirtiness). So the F-Book this is not. (The fact that an early computer science book on compiler-writing was called the Dragon Book, for the sole reason that someone had [I suppose arbitrarily] put the picture of a dragon on its cover, didn't cut any ice in this particular matter.)

But in my defense, I would like to say this: Each of those F-words was there for a purpose, to carry its weight in the gathering meaning of the title. The *55*, of course, was just a gimmick. I aimed for 55 facts because that would add to the alliteration in the title. (Alan Davis's wonderful book of 201 principles of software engineering was just as arbitrary in its striving for 201, I'll bet.) But the rest of the *F*s were carefully chosen.

Frequently forgotten? Because most of them are. There's a lot of stuff in here that you will be able to say "oh, yeah, I remember that one" and then muse about why you forgot it over the years.

Fundamental? The primary reason for choosing this particular collection of facts is because all of them carry major significance in the software field. We may have forgotten many of them, but that doesn't diminish their importance. In fact, if you're still wondering whether to go on reading this book, the most important reason I can give you for continuing is that I strongly believe that, in this collection of facts, you will find the most fundamentally important knowledge in the software engineering field.

Facts? Oddly, this is probably the most controversial of the words in the title. You may not agree with all of the facts I have chosen here. You may even violently disagree with some of them. I personally believe that they all represent fact, but that doesn't mean you have to.

A few fallacies? There are some sacred cows in the software field that I just couldn't resist skewering! I suppose I have to admit that the things I call fallacies are things that others might call facts. But part of your fun in reading this book should be forming your own opinion on the things I call facts—and the things I call fallacies.

How about the age of these facts and fallacies? One reviewer of this book said that parts of it felt dated. Guilty as charged. For facts and fallacies to be forgotten frequently, they must have been around for awhile. There are plenty of golden oldies in this collection. But here I think you will find some facts and fallacies that will surprise you, as well—ideas that are "new" because you're not familiar with them. The point of these facts and fallacies is not that they are aged. It's that they are ageless.

In this part of the book, I want to introduce the facts that follow. The fallacies will have their own introduction later in the book. My idea of an introduction is to take one last trip through these 55 frequently forgotten fundamental facts and see how many of them track with all of those F-words. Putting on my objectivity hat, I have to admit that some of these facts aren't all that forgotten.

- Twelve of the facts are simply little known. They haven't been forgotten; many people haven't heard of them. But they are, I would assert, fundamentally important.
- Eleven of them are pretty well accepted, but no one seems to act on them.
- Eight of them are accepted, but we don't agree on how—or whether—to fix the problems they represent.
- Six of them are probably totally accepted by most people, with no controversy and little forgetting.
- Five of them, many people will flat-out disagree with.
- Five of them are accepted by many people, but a few wildly disagree, making them quite controversial.

That doesn't add up to 55 because (a) some of the facts could fit into multiple categories, and (b) there were some trace presences of other categories, like "only vendors would disagree with this." Rather than telling you which facts fit into which of those categories, I think I'll let you form your own opinion about them.

There's controversy galore in this book, as you can see. To help deal with that, following each discussion about a fact, I acknowledge the controversies surrounding it. I hope, by doing that, I will cover your viewpoint, whether it matches mine or not, and allow you to see where what you believe fits with what I believe.

Given the amount of controversy I've admitted to, it probably would be wise of me to tell you my credentials for selecting these facts and engaging in this controversy. (There's a humorous bio in the back of the book, so here I'll make it quick.) I've been in the software engineering field for over 45 years, mostly as a technical practitioner and researcher. I've written 25 books and more than 75 professional papers on the subject. I have regular columns in three of the leading journals in the field: The Practical Programmer in *Communications of the ACM,* The Loyal Opposition in *IEEE Software,* and Through a Glass, Darkly in ACM's SIGMIS *DATABASE.* I'm known as a contrarian, and I have a plaque identifying me as the "Premier Curmudgeon of Software Practice" to prove it! You can count on me to question the unquestionable and, as I said earlier, to skewer a few sacred cows.

There's one additional thing I'd like to say about these facts. I've already said that I carefully picked them to make sure they were all fundamental to the field. But for all my questioning about how many of them are really forgotten, nearly all of them represent knowledge that we fail to act on. Managers of practitioners make proclamations showing that they've forgotten or never heard of many of them. Software developers work in a world too constrained by their lack of knowledge of them. Researchers advocate things that they would realize are absurd if they were to consider them. I really do believe that there's a rich learning experience—or a rich remembering experience—for those of you who choose to read on.

Now, before I turn you loose among the facts, I want to set some important expectations. In presenting these facts, in many cases, I am also identifying problems in the field. It is not my intention here to present solutions to those problems. This is a what-is book, not a how-to book. That's important to me; what I want to achieve here is to bring these facts back into the open, where they can be freely discussed and progress toward acting on them can be made. I think that's an important enough goal that I don't want to dilute it by diverting the discussion to solutions. Solutions for the problems represented by these facts are often found in books and papers already published in our field: software engineering textbooks, specialty topic software engineering books, the leading software engineering journals, and software popular-press magazines (although there is profound ignorance mixed in with important information in many of these).

To help with that quest, I present these facts in the following orchestrated structure:

- First, I *discuss* the fact.
- Then I present the *controversies,* if any, surrounding the fact.
- And finally, I present the *sources* of information regarding the fact, a bibliography of background and foreground information. Many of those sources are ancient, by software engineering standards (those are the frequently forgotten facts). Many are as fresh as tomorrow. Some are both.

I've aggregated my 55 facts into several categories: those that are

- About management
- About the life cycle
- About quality
- About research

The fallacies are aggregated similarly:

- About management
- About the life cycle
- About education

Ah, enough preparation. I hope you'll enjoy the facts and fallacies I present here. And, more important, I hope you'll find them useful.

Robert L. Glass
Summer 2002

CHAPTER 1

About Management

To tell you the truth, I've always thought management was kind of a boring subject. Judging by the books I've read on the subject, it's 95 percent common sense and 5 percent warmed-over advice from yester-decade. So why am I leading off this book with the topic of management?

Because, to give the devil its due, most of the high-leverage, high-visibility things that happen in the software field are about management. Most of our failures, for example, are blamed on management. And most of our successes can be attributed to management. In Al Davis's wonderful book on software principles (1995), he says it very clearly in Principle 127: "Good management is more important than good technology." Much as I hate to admit it, Al is right.

Why do I hate to admit it? Early in my career, I faced the inevitable fork in the road. I could remain a technologist, continuing to do what I loved to do—building software, or I could take the other fork and become a manager. I thought about it pretty hard. The great American way involves moving up the ladder of success, and it was difficult to think of avoiding that ladder. But, in the end, two things made me realize I didn't want to leave my technology behind.

1. I wanted to *do*, not *direct others* to do.

2. I wanted to be free to make my own decisions, not become a "manager in the middle" who often had to pass on the decisions of those above him.

The latter thing may strike you as odd. How can a technologist remain more free to make decisions than his or her manager? I knew that, from my own experience, it was true, but it was tough explaining it to others. I finally wrote a whole book on the subject, *The Power of Peonage* (1979). The essence of that book—and my belief that led to my remaining a technologist—is that those people who are really good at what they do and yet are at the bottom of a management hierarchy have a power that no one else in the hierarchy has. They can't be demoted. As peons, there is often no lower rank for them to be relegated to. It may be possible to threaten a good technologist with some sort of punishment, but being moved down the hierarchy isn't one of those ways. And I found myself using that power many times during my technical years.

But I digress. The subject here is why I, a deliberate nonmanager-type, chose to lead off this book with the topic of management. Well, what I want to say here is that being a technologist was more *fun* than being a manager. I didn't say it was more *important*. In fact, probably the most vitally important of software's frequently forgotten facts are management things. Unfortunately, managers often get so enmeshed in all that commonsense, warmed-over advice that they lose sight of some very specific and, what ought to be very memorable and certainly vitally important, facts.

Like things about people. How important they are. How some are astonishingly better than others. How projects succeed or fail primarily based on who does the work rather than how it's done.

Like things about tools and techniques (which, after all, are usually chosen by management). How hype about them does more harm than good. How switching to new approaches diminishes before it enhances. How seldom new tools and techniques are really used.

Like things about estimation. How bad our estimates so often are. How awful the process of obtaining them is. How we equate failure to achieve those bad estimates with other, much more important kinds of project failure. How management and technologists have achieved a "disconnect" over estimation.

Like things about reuse. How long we've been doing reuse. How little reuse has progressed in recent years. How much hope some people place (probably erroneously) on reuse.

Like things about complexity. How the complexity of building software accounts for so many of the problems of the field. How quickly complexity can ramp up. How it takes pretty bright people to overcome this complexity.

There! That's a quick overview of the chapter that lies ahead. Let's proceed into the facts that are so frequently forgotten, and so important to remember, in the subject matter covered by the term *management*.

References

➥ Davis, Alan M. 1995. *201 Principles of Software Development.* New York: McGraw-Hill.

➥ Glass, Robert L. 1979. *The Power of Peonage.* Computing Trends.

PEOPLE

Fact 1	The most important factor in software work is *not* the tools and techniques used by the programmers, but rather the quality of the programmers themselves.

Discussion

People matter in building software. That's the message of this particular fact. Tools matter. Techniques also matter. Process, yet again, matters. But head and shoulders above all those other things that matter are people.

This message is as old as the software field itself. It has emerged from, and appears in, so many software research studies and position papers over the years that, by now, it should be one of the most important software "eternal truths." Yet we in the software field keep forgetting it. We advocate process as the be-all and end-all of software development. We promote tools as breakthroughs in our ability to create software. We aggregate a miscellaneous collection of techniques, call that aggregate a methodology, and insist that thousands of programmers read about it, take classes in it, have their noses rubbed in it through drill and practice, and then employ it on high-profile projects. All in the name of tools/techniques/process over people.

We even revert, from time to time, to anti-people approaches. We treat people like interchangeable cogs on an assembly line. We claim that people work better when too-tight schedules and too-binding constraints are imposed on them. We deny our programmers even the most fundamental elements of trust and then expect them to trust us in telling them what to do.

In this regard, it is interesting to look at the Software Engineering Institute (SEI) and its software process, the Capability Maturity Model. The CMM assumes that good process is the way to good software. It lays out a plethora of key process areas and a set of stair steps through which software organizations are urged to progress, all based on that fundamental assumption. What makes the CMM particularly interesting is that after a few years of its existence and after it had been semi-institutionalized by the U.S. Department of Defense as a way of improving software organizations and after others had copied the DoD's approaches, only then did the SEI begin to examine people and their importance in building software. There is now an SEI People Capability Maturity Model. But it is far less well known and far less well utilized than the process CMM. Once again, in the minds of many software engineering professionals, process is more important than people, sometimes spectacularly more important. It seems as if we will never learn.

Controversy

The controversy regarding the importance of people is subtle. Everyone pays lip service to the notion that people are important. Nearly everyone agrees, at a superficial level, that people trump tools, techniques, and process. And yet we keep behaving as if it were not true. Perhaps it's because people are a harder problem to address than tools, techniques, and process. Perhaps it's like one of those "little moron" jokes. (In one sixty-year-old joke in that series, a little moron seems to be looking for something under a lamp post. When asked what he is doing, he replies "I lost my keys." "Where did you lose them?" he is asked. "Over there," says the little moron, pointing off to the side. "Then why are you looking under the lamp post?" "Because," says the little moron, "the light is better here.")

We in the software field, all of us technologists at heart, would prefer to invent new technologies to make our jobs easier. Even if we know, deep down inside, that the people issue is a more important one to work.

 ## Sources

The most prominent expression of the importance of people comes from the front cover illustration of Barry Boehm's classic book *Software Engineering Economics* (1981). There, he lays out a bar chart of the factors that contribute to doing a good job of software work. And, lo and behold, the longest bar on the chart represents the quality of the people doing the work. People, the chart tells us, are far more important than whatever tools, techniques, languages, and—yes—processes those people are using.

Perhaps the most important expression of this point is the also-classic book *Peopleware* (DeMarco and Lister 1999). As you might guess from the title, the entire book is about the importance of people in the software field. It says things like "The major problems of our work are not so much technological as sociological in nature" and goes so far as to say that looking at technology first is a "High-Tech Illusion." You can't read *Peopleware* without coming away with the belief that people matter a whole lot more than any other factor in the software field.

The most succinct expression of the importance of people is in Davis (1995), where the author states simply, "People are the key to success." The most recent expressions of the importance of people come from the Agile Development movement, where people say things like "Peel back the facade of rigorous methodology projects and ask why the project was successful, and the answer [is] people" (Highsmith 2002). And the earliest expressions of the importance of people come from authors like Bucher (1975), who said, "The prime factor in affecting the reliability of software is in the selection, motivation, and management of the personnel who design and maintain it," and Rubey (1978), who said, "When all is said and done, the ultimate factor in software productivity is the capability of the individual software practitioner."

But perhaps my favorite place where people were identified as the most important factor in software work was an obscure article on a vitally important issue. The issue was, "If your life depended on a particular piece of software, what would you want to know about it?" Bollinger responded, "More than anything else, I would want to know that the person who wrote the software was both highly intelligent, and possessed by an extremely rigorous, almost fanatical desire to make their program work the way it should. Everything else to me is secondary. . . ." (2001).

References

➥ Boehm, Barry. 1981. *Software Engineering Economics.* Englewood Cliffs, NJ: Prentice-Hall.

➥ Bollinger, Terry. 2001. "On Inspection vs. Testing." *Software Practitioner,* Sept.

➥ Bucher, D. E. W. 1975. "Maintenance of the Computer Sciences Teleprocessing System." Proceedings of the International Conference on Reliable Software, Seattle, WA, April.

➥ Davis, Alan M. 1995. *201 Principles of Software Development.* New York: McGraw-Hill.

➥ DeMarco, Tom, and Timothy Lister. 1999. *Peopleware.* 2d ed. New York: Dorset House.

➥ Highsmith, James A. 2002. *Agile Software Development Ecosystems.* Boston: Addison-Wesley.

➥ Rubey, Raymond L. 1978. "Higher Order Languages for Avionics Software—A Survey, Summary, and Critique." Proceedings of NAECON.

Fact 2	The best programmers are up to 28 times better than the worst programmers, according to "individual differences" research. Given that their pay is never commensurate, they are the biggest bargains in the software field.

 ### Discussion

The point of the previous fact was that people matter in building software. The point of this fact is that they matter a lot!

This is another message that is as old as the software field. In fact, the sources I cite date mostly back to 1968–1978. It is almost as if we have known this fundamental fact so well and for so long that it sort of slides effortlessly out of our memory.

The significance of this fact is profound. Given how much better some software practitioners are than others—and we will see numbers ranging from 5 times better to 28 times better—it is fairly obvious that the care and feeding of the best people we have is the most important task of the software manager. In fact, those 28-to-1 people—who probably are being paid considerably less than double their not-so-good peers—are the best bargains in software. (For that matter, so are those 5-to-1 folks.)

The problem is—and of course there is a problem, since we are not acting on this fact in our field—we don't know how to identify those "best" people. We have struggled over the years with programmer aptitude tests and certified data processor exams and the ACM self-assessment programs, and the bottom line, after a lot of blood and sweat and perhaps even tears were spent on them, was that the correlation between test scores and on-the-job performance is nil. (You think that was disappointing? We also learned, about that time, that computer science class grades and on-the-job performance correlated abysmally also [Sackman 1968].)

Controversy

The controversy surrounding this fact is simply that we fail to grasp its significance. I have never heard anyone doubt the truth of the matter. We simply forget that the importance of this particular fact is considerably more than academic.

Sources

I promised a plethora of "old-time" references in this matter. Here goes.

- "The most important practical finding [of our study] involves the striking individual differences in programmer performance" (Sackman 1968). The researchers had found differences of up to 28 to 1 while trying to evaluate the productivity difference between batch and timesharing computer usage. (The individual differences made it nearly impossible for them to do an effective comparison of usage approaches.)

- "Within a group of programmers, there may be an order of magnitude difference in capability" (Schwartz 1968). Schwartz was studying the problems of developing large-scale software.

- "Productivity variations of 5:1 between individuals are common" (Boehm 1975). Boehm was exploring what he termed "the high cost of software."

- "There is a tremendous amount of variability in the individual results. For instance, two people . . . found only one error, but five people found seven errors. The variability among student programmers is well known, but the high variability among these highly experienced subjects was somewhat surprising" (Myers 1978). Myers did the early definitive studies on software reliability methodologies.

These quotations and the data they contain are so powerful that I feel no need to augment what those early authors learned, except to say that I see no reason to believe that this particular finding—and fact—would have changed over time. But let me add a couple of more quotations from the Al Davis book (1995) "Principle 132—A few good people are better than many less skilled people" and "Principle 141—There are huge differences among software engineers."

And here is a more recent source: McBreen (2002) suggests paying "great developers" "what they're worth" ($150K to $250K), and lesser ones much less.

References

➥ Boehm, Barry. 1975. "The High Cost of Software." *Practical Strategies for Developing Large Software Systems*, edited by Ellis Horowitz. Reading, MA: Addison-Wesley.

➥ Glass, Robert L. 1995. *Software Creativity*. Englewood Cliffs, NJ: Prentice-Hall.

➥ McBreen, Pete. 2002. *Software Craftsmanship*. Boston: Addison-Wesley.

➥ Myers, Glenford. 1978. "A Controlled Experiment in Program Testing and Code Walkthroughs/Inspections." *Communications of the ACM,* Sept.

➥ Sackman, H., W. I. Erikson, and E. E. Grant. 1968. "Exploratory Experimental Studies Comparing Online and Offline Programming Performances." *Communications of the ACM,* Jan.

➥ Schwartz, Jules. 1968. "Analyzing Large-Scale System Development." In *Software Engineering Concepts and Techniques,* Proceedings of the 1968 NATO Conference, edited by Thomas Smith and Karen Billings. New York: Petrocelli/Charter.

Fact 3	Adding people to a late project makes it later.

 ### Discussion

This is one of the classic facts of software engineering. In fact, it is more than a fact, it is a law—"Brooks's law" (1995).

Intuition tells us that, if a project is behind schedule, staffing should be increased to play schedule catch-up. Intuition, this fact tells us, is wrong. The problem is, as people are added to a project, time must be spent on bringing them up to speed. They have a lot to learn before they can become productive. But more important, those things they must learn typically must be acquired from the others on the project team. The result is that the new team members are very slow to contribute anything to the project at all, and while they are becoming productive, they are a drain on the time and attention of the existing project team.

Furthermore, the more people there are on a project, the more the complexity of its communications rises. Thus adding these new people when a project is late tends to make it even later.

Controversy

Most people acknowledge the correctness of this fact. At the same time, it is possible to argue with some of the details. For example, what if the added people are already knowledgeable in this application domain, and perhaps even on this project? Then the learning curve problem diminishes, and the newcomers may end up contributing quite rapidly. Or what if the project is barely under way? In that case, there's not that much to bring the added people up to speed.

The opposition to the fact is best articulated by McConnell (1999), who notes that (a) ignoring the fact "remains commonplace" in practice, and (b) the fact is valid only in "limited circumstances that are easily identified and avoided."

Still, few dispute the fundamental fact here. One must be very careful in adding staff to a behind-schedule project. (For that matter, one must be careful in adding staff to any project, late or not. But it's especially tempting—and especially dangerous—when the manager is trying to accelerate progress.)

Sources

This fact accounts for the title of a classic software engineering book. The book is called *The Mythical Man-Month* (Brooks 1995) because, although we tend to measure staffing in people per month, not all people contribute the same amount to a project, and thus not all man-months are equal. This is especially true for those people added to a late project, whose man-month contribution may very well be negative.

➡ Brooks, Frederick P., Jr. 1995. *The Mythical Man-Month.* Anniversary ed. Reading MA: Addison-Wesley.

➡ McConnell, Steve. 1999. "Brooks' Law Repealed." From the Editor. *IEEE Software*, Nov.

Fact 4	The working environment has a profound impact on productivity and product quality.

Discussion

The tendency in software projects is to try to staff them with the best people available, enlist the support of an appropriate methodology, establish a process fairly high up on the SEI CMM food chain, and let 'er rip! The problem is, there's something important left out of that mix. The setting in which the systems analysts analyze and the designers design and the programmers program and the testers test—that environment matters a lot. A whole lot.

What it all boils down to is that software work is thought-intensive, and the environment in which it is done must be one that facilitates thinking. Crowding and the resulting (intentional or unintentional) interruptions are deadly to making progress.

How deadly? There's a whole classic book that focuses on this issue. *Peopleware* (DeMarco and Lister 1999) spends quite a bit of its time and space telling us just how, and in what ways, the environment matters. In it, the authors report on their own studies of the effect of the work environment on job performance. They took members of a project team and separated the top quartile of performers from the bottom quartile (the top quartile performed 2.6 times better than those at the bottom). They then examined the working environment of those people at the top and those at the bottom. The top people had 1.7 times as much workspace (measured in available floor space in square feet). Twice as often, they found their workspace "acceptably quiet." More than 3 times as often, they found it "acceptably private." Between 4 and 5 times as often, they could divert phone calls or silence their phone. They were interrupted by other people (needlessly) about half as often.

It is certainly true that the individual differences between people have a profound effect on software productivity, as we have already seen in Fact 2. But this fact tells us that there is something more needed. You must get good people, and then you must treat them well, especially in providing a workable environment.

Controversy

The controversy here is underground. Hardly anyone will disagree with this fact publicly. And yet when the time comes to provide office space, the field seems to revert to its old "crowd them in as closely as possible" philosophy. The money spent on additional office space is easily measured and easily manipulated, whereas the cost to productivity and quality by crowding software people into too little space is much harder to measure.

Workers say things like "you never get anything done around here" (that's the title of one of *Peopleware*'s chapters, in fact). Managers give authority on defining workspace matters to people who think as if they were "the furniture police" (that's another of its chapter titles). And yet very little seems to change. Even in the academic world, where thinking time is valued more than in most settings, the pressure of too little space for too many people often results in crowded or doubled-up offices.

There is an old saying, "the hard drives out the soft." That is, those things that are solidly measurable ("hard" things) tend to take attention away from those that are not (the "soft" ones). This truism is about much more than software, but it seems especially relevant here. Office space measurement is hard. Productive benefits are soft. Guess which one wins?

There is one burgeoning controversy connected to this fact. Advocates of Extreme Programming argue for a way of working called pair programming. In pair programming, two software workers stay in close communication and proximity while they are doing their work, even sharing use of the computer keyboard. Here, we see intentional crowding, yet with the attendant claim that productivity and especially quality benefit. The controversy between these two viewpoints has not yet been articulated in the software literature, but as Extreme Programming becomes better known, this controversy may hit the fan.

 ## Sources

There are several sources of information on Extreme Programming, but here is the first and best known:

➡ Beck, Kent. 2000. *Extreme Programming Explained.* Boston: Addison-Wesley.

One leading advocate of pair programming, Laurie Williams, has written about it in many places, including the following:

➡ Williams, Laurie, Robert Kessler, Ward Cunningham, and Ron Jeffries. 2000. "Strengthening the Case for Pair Programming." *IEEE Software* 17, no. 4

 ## Reference

➡ DeMarco, Tom, and Timothy Lister. 1999. *Peopleware.* 2d ed. New York: Dorset House.

TOOLS AND TECHNIQUES

Fact 5	Hype is the plague on the house of software. Most software tool and technique improvements account for about a 5 to 35 percent increase in productivity and quality. But at one time or another, most of those same improvements have been claimed by someone to have "order of magnitude" benefits.

 ## Discussion

Time was, way back when, that new software engineering ideas were really breakthroughs. High-order programming languages. Automated tools like debuggers. General-purpose operating systems. That was then (the 1950s). This is now. The era of breakthrough techniques, the things that Fred Brooks (1987) referred to as silver bullets, is long since over.

Oh, we may have fourth-generation languages ("programming without programmers") and CASE tools ("the automation of programming) and object orientation ("the best way to build software") and Extreme Programming ("the future of the field") and whatever the breakthrough du jour is. But, in spite of the blather surrounding their announcement and advocacy, those things are simply not that dramatically helpful in our ability to build software. And, to paraphrase Brooks himself, the most rational viewpoint to take on breakthroughs is "not now, not ever." Or perhaps, "unlikely ever again."

In fact, there is some pretty solid data to that effect. Nearly all so-called breakthroughs, circa 1970 to today, are good for modest benefits (less than 35 percent) for software engineers. Considering that the breakthrough blather is making claims for "order of magnitude" improvements (that is, powers of 10), there is a huge gap between these claims and reality.

The evidence on this subject is quite strong. In my own longitudinal research, examining evaluative studies by objective researchers of the value of these improvements (Glass 1999), I have found

- A serious lack of evaluative research because there are few such studies to draw on.

- Enough studies to be able to draw some significant conclusions.

- A nearly total lack of any evidence that any of these things has breakthrough benefits.

- Fairly solid evidence that the benefits are indeed there, but at a far more modest level—5 to 35 percent.

(The references and further readings in that paper can point you to the original studies that produced this objective evaluative data.)

These findings are echoed in a wonderful table in a best of practice book on software process improvement (Grady 1997), in which the author lists some of the various process changes that are part of a process improvement program and the benefits that may be achieved by them. What was the highest benefit process change, you may ask? Reuse. The payoff for reuse, according to Grady, is 10 to 35 percent. Contrast that with the extravagant "order of magnitude" claims of the componentry zealots of today. Or the claims of any of the other zealots of yesteryear.

Why do we go through this cycle of hype-and-dashed-hopes again and again? It takes two kinds of people to sustain this cycle—the hypesters themselves and the true believers. The hypesters, as it turns out, almost always are nonobjective folks who have something to gain—product sales, high-priced courses, or funding for research projects. 'Twas always thus. Since the days of the Universal Elixir peddlers, there have always been people eager to make a fast buck on promises unsubstantiable by realities.

The ones who worry me, given that there will always be fast-buck pursuers, are those true believers. Why do those folks believe, again and again and again, the promises of the hypesters? Why are we subjected, again and again and again, to massive expenditure and training in new concepts that cannot possibly deliver what is claimed for them? Answering that question is one of the most important tasks of our field. If answering it were easy, we wouldn't have to ask it. But I will try to suggest answers in the material that follows.

Controversy

I've never met anyone who disagreed with the notion that there is too much hype in the software field. But behavior, all too often, clashes with this belief. Nearly everyone, at the conceptual level, agrees with the Brooks notion that there is unlikely to be any silver bullet forthcoming. But so many people, when push really gets down to shove, leap eagerly aboard the latest software engineering breakthrough bandwagon.

Sometimes I think what is happening is a kind of "hardware envy." Our computer hardware brethren have made remarkable progress in the few decades that computer hardware has been produced. Cheaper/better/faster happens over and over again in that hardware world. Friends who study the history of technology tell me that progress in the computer hardware field is probably faster than that in any other field, ever. Perhaps we in software are so envious of that progress that we pretend that it is happening—or can happen—to us.

There is another thing going on, as well. Because the whole hardware/software thing has moved forward so dramatically and so rapidly, there is a great fear of being left behind and a great eagerness to participate in whatever is new. We draw up life cycles of new process/product innovation, and cheer for the "early adopters" while booing the "laggards." In the computing field there is a whole cultural thing that says new is better than old. Given all of that, who indeed would not want to embrace the new and step away from the old? In that emotional climate, buying into hype is a good thing, and stepping up in front of the hype steamroller is bad.

What a shame all of that is. The software field has been victimized so many times by its hypesters and their fellow travelers. And, to make matters worse, I'd be willing to bet that—as you are reading this—there is some other new idea parading down the pike, its zealots leading the way and claiming dramatic bene-fits, your colleagues dancing merrily along in their wake. The Pied Piper of hype is striking yet again!

 Sources

The pronouncements of the fact of hype are severely outnumbered by the purvey-ors of faulty promise. I can't remember back far enough to identify the first pub-lished hypester, and I wouldn't want to give them "credit" here if I could. But it has all been going on for a very long time. My very first book (1976), for example, was titled *The Universal Elixir, and Other Computing Projects Which Failed* and told a few tales that ridiculed these computing elixir-selling hypesters. Those stories had originally been published in *Computerworld* (under an assumed name, Miles Benson) for a decade before they were gathered into that book.

There are far more sources that promise panaceas then there are voices of reason crying in this wilderness. But here, as well as in the References that follow, are a few of those voices:

➡ Davis, Alan M. 1995. *201 Principles of Software Development.* New York: McGraw-Hill. Principle 129 is "Don't believe everything you read."

➡ Weinberg, Gerald. 1992. *Quality Software Development: Systems Thinking.* Vol. 1, p. 291. New York: Dorset House.

 References

➡ Brooks, Frederick P., Jr. 1987. "No Silver Bullet—Essence and Accidents of Software Engineering." *IEEE Computer,* Apr. This paper has been published in several other places, most notably in the Anniversary Edition of Brooks's best-known book, *The Mythical Man-Month* (Reading, MA: Addison-Wesley, 1995), where it is not only included in its original form but updated.

➡ Glass, Robert L. 1976. "The Universal Elixir, and Other Computing Projects Which Failed." *Computerworld.* Republished by Computing Trends, 1977, 1979, 1981, and 1992.

➡ Glass, Robert L. 1999. "The Realities of Software Technology Payoffs." *Communications of the ACM,* Feb.

➡ Grady, Robert B. 1997. *Successful Software Process Improvement.* Table 4-1, p. 69. Englewood Cliffs, NJ: Prentice-Hall.

> **Fact 6** Learning a new tool or technique actually lowers programmer productivity and product quality initially. The eventual benefit is achieved only after this learning curve is overcome. Therefore, it is worth adopting new tools and techniques, but only (a) if their value is seen realistically and (b) if patience is used in measuring benefits.

 ## Discussion

Learning a new tool or technique, assuming that there is value associated with its use, is a good thing. But perhaps not as good as the early adopters might have us believe. There is a cost to learning to use new ideas. We must come to understand the new idea, see how it fits into what we do, decide how to apply it, and consider when it should and shouldn't be used. Being forced to think about things that previously have been pretty automatic for us slows us down.

Whether the new idea is using a test coverage analyzer tool for the first time and figuring out what that means to our testing process or trying out Extreme Programming and adjusting to all the new techniques it contains, the user of the new idea will be less efficient and less effective. That does not mean that these new ideas should be avoided; it simply means that the first project on which they are employed will go more slowly, not faster, than usual.

Improving productivity and product quality have been the holy grails of software process for the last couple of decades. The reason we adopt new tools and techniques is to improve productivity and quality. So it is an irony of the technology transfer process that productivity and quality initially go down, not up, when we change gears and try something new.

Not to worry. If there truly is benefit to the new thing, eventually it will emerge. But that brings up the question "how long?" What we are talking about is the learning curve. In the learning curve, efficiency and effectiveness dip at the outset, rise back past the norm, and eventually plateau at whatever benefit the new thing is capable of achieving. Given that, the "how long" question translates into several "how longs." How long will we have diminished benefits? How soon do we return to normal benefits? How long before we get the ultimate benefits?

At this point, what all of us would like to be able to say is something like "three months" and "six months." But, of course, none of us can say that—or anything else, for that matter. The length of the learning curve is situation- and environment-dependent. Often, the higher the benefit at the end, the longer the learning curve. To learn object orientation superficially might take three months, but to become proficient at it might take two fully immersed years. For other things, the lengths would be totally different. The only predictable thing is that there will be a learning curve. One can draw the curve on a chart, but one cannot put any meaningful scale on that chart's axes.

The one remaining question is "how much?" How much benefit will the new idea bring us? That is just as unknowable as the answers to the "how long" questions. Except for one thing. Because of what we learned in the previous fact, it is most likely true that the benefit will be 5 to 35 percent higher than was achieved before the new idea was assimilated.

There is one more important factor to add. Although we cannot give any general answers to the "how long" and "how much" questions, there are answers. For any new concept—test coverage analyzers or Extreme Programming, for example—those with experience can help you with those questions. Find people who already have assimilated the concept you want to embrace, through your peer network, user group, professional society, and so on, and inquire about how long it took them (they are quite likely to know the answer to that question) and how much benefit they achieved (that's a tougher question, and unless they are users of software metrics approaches, they may not know). And don't forget, while you're asking, to find out what lessons they learned—pro and con—in their adoption process.

Be sure to avoid zealots when you ask those questions, of course. Zealots sometimes give the answers they believe, rather than the answers they experienced.

Controversy

There shouldn't be any controversy over this matter. It is obvious that there is cost attached to learning something new. But, in fact, there often is controversy. The claims of zealots for huge benefits and quick learning curves all too often translate into management belief in those benefits and in that quick learning process (see Fact 5). Managers expect new approaches, when employed, to work right out of the box. Under those circumstances, cost and schedule estimates are made with the assumption that the benefits will be achieved from the beginning.

In a classic story to this effect, one pharmaceutical company, installing the SAP megapackage, bid low on some contracts because they assumed the benefits of SAP would be achieved immediately. That company disappeared, a learning curve period later, in a flame of bankruptcy and litigation. "Don't try this at home" might be the lesson learned here.

Source

The learning curve and its impact on progress is described in many places, including

➡ Weinberg, Gerald. 1997. *Quality Software Management: Anticipating Change.* Vol. 4, pp. 13, 20. New York: Dorset House.

Fact 7	Software developers talk a lot about tools. They evaluate quite a few, buy a fair number, and use practically none.

Discussion

Tools are the toys of the software developer. They love to learn about new tools, try them out, even procure them. And then something funny happens. The tools seldom get used.

A colorful term emerged from this tendency a decade or so ago. During the height of the CASE tools movement, when everyone seemed to believe that CASE tools were the way of the software future, a way that might well automate the process of software development, lots and lots of those CASE tools were purchased. But so many of them were put on the figurative shelf and never used, that the term *shelfware* was invented to describe the phenomenon.

I was a victim of that whole movement. At the time, I frequently taught a seminar on software quality. In that seminar, I expressed my own belief that those CASE tools were nowhere near the breakthrough technology that others claimed them to be. Some of my students sought me out after one session to tell me that I was out-of-date on the subject of CASE. They were convinced, as I was not, that these tools were indeed capable of automating the software development process.

I took those students seriously and immediately immersed myself in the CASE body of knowledge to make sure that I hadn't indeed missed something and become out-of-date. Time passed. And along with the passage of time came vindication for my point of view. CASE tools were indeed beneficial, we soon learned, but they were definitely not magical breakthroughs. The shelfware phenomenon resulted, among other things, from those dashed hopes.

But I digress. This fact is not about tools seen to be breakthroughs (we skewered that thought in Fact 5), but rather tools as successful productivity enhancers. And, for the most part, they are that. So why do these kinds of tools also end up on the shelf?

Remember Fact 6 about the learning curve? The one that says that trying out a new tool or technique, far from immediately improving productivity, actually diminishes it at the outset? Once the thrill of trying out a new tool has worn off, the poor schedule-driven software developer must build real software to real schedules. And, all too often, the developer reverts to what he or she knows best, the same tools always used. Compilers for the well-known programming language they know and love. Debuggers for that language. Their favorite (probably language-independent) text editors. Linkers and loaders that do your bidding almost without your thinking about it. Last year's (or last decade's) configuration management tools. Isn't that enough tools to fill your toolbox? Never mind coverage analyzers or conditional compilers or standards-conformance checkers or whatever the tool du jour might be. They might be fun to play with, these developers say to themselves, but they're a drag when it comes to being productive.

There is another problem about tools in the software field, in addition to the one we have already discussed. There is no "minimum standard toolset," a definition of the collection of tools that all programmers should have in their toolboxes. If there were such a definition, programmers would be much more likely to use at least the tools that made up that set. This is a problem that no one seems to be working on. (At one time, IBM proposed a toolset called AD/Cycle, but it made a dull thud in the marketplace—it was too expensive and too poorly thought through—and no one has tried to do that since.)

Controversy

Often software practitioners are tagged with the "not-invented-here" (NIH) phenomenon. They are accused of preferring to do their own thing rather than building on the work of others.

There is, of course, some of that in the field. But there is not as much as many seem to think. Most programmers I know, given the choice of something new or something old, will use the something new, but only if they are sure that they can complete their tasks at hand more quickly if they do. Since that is seldom the case (there's that old learning curve problem again), they revert to the old, the tried, the true.

The problem here, I would assert, is not NIH. The problem is a culture that puts schedule conformance, using impossible schedules, above all else—a culture that values schedule so highly that there is no time to learn about new concepts. There are tools catalogs (for example, ACR) that describe the what/where/how of commercial tools. Few programmers are aware of the existence of many of the tools of our trade. Fewer still are aware of the catalogs that could lead to them. We will return to these thoughts in the facts that follow.

Regarding any controversy over a minimum standard toolset, so few are giving that any thought that there is no controversy whatsoever. Imagine what wonderful controversy could result if people began thinking about it.

Sources

➡ ACR. The ACR Library of Programmer's and Developer's Tools, Applied Computer Research, Inc., P.O. Box 82266, Phoenix AZ 85071-2266. This was an annually updated software tools catalog, but has suspended publication recently.

➡ Glass, Robert L. 1991. "Recommended: A Minimum Standard Software Toolset." In *Software Conflict.* Englewood Cliffs, NJ: Yourdon Press.

➡ Wiegers, Karl. 2001. Personal communication. Wiegers says, "This fact is something I've said repeatedly. It has been published in an interview I once did, conducted by David Rubinstein and appearing in *Software Development Times,* Oct. 15, 2000."

ESTIMATION

Fact 8	One of the two most common causes of runaway projects is poor estimation. (For the other, see Fact 23, page 67.)

Discussion

Runaway projects are those that spiral out of control. All too often, they fail to produce any product at all. If they do, whatever they produce will be well behind schedule and well over budget. Along the way, there is lots of wreckage, both in corporate and human terms. Some projects are known as "death marches." Others are said to operate in "crunch mode." Whatever they are called, whatever the result, runaway projects are not a pretty sight.

The question of what causes such runaways arises frequently in the software engineering field. The answer to the question, all too often, is based on the personal biases of the person who is answering the question. Some say a lack of proper methodology causes runaways; often, those people are selling some kind of methodology. Some say it is a lack of good tools (guess what those people do for a living?). Some say it is a lack of discipline and rigor among programmers (typically, the methodologies being advocated and often sold by those people are based on heavy doses of imposed discipline). Name an advocated concept, someone is saying the lack of it is what causes runaway projects.

In the midst of this clamor and chaos, fortunately, there are some genuinely objective answers to the question, answers from which typically no one stands to gain by whatever comes of the answer. And those answers are fascinatingly consistent: The two causes of runaways that stand head and shoulders above all others are poor (usually optimistic) estimation and unstable requirements. One of them leads in some research studies, and the other in other studies.

In this section of the book, I want to focus on estimation. (I will cover unstable requirements later.) Estimation, as you might imagine, is the process by which we determine how long a project will take and how much it will cost. We do estimation very badly in the software field. Most of our estimates are more like wishes than realistic targets. To make matters worse, we seem to have no idea how to improve on those very bad practices. And the result is, as everyone tries to meet an impossible estimation target, shortcuts are taken, good practices are skipped, and the inevitable schedule runaway becomes a technology runaway as well.

We have tried all kinds of apparently reasonable approaches to improve on our ability to estimate. To begin with, we relied on "expert" people, software developers who had "been there and done that." The problem with that approach is it's very subjective. Different people with different "been there and done that" experiences produce different estimates. In fact, whatever it was that those people had been and done before was unlikely to be sufficiently similar to the present problem to extrapolate well. (One of the important factors that characterizes software projects is the vast differences among the problems they solve. We will elaborate on that thought later.)

Then we tried algorithmic approaches. Computer scientists tend to be mathematicians at heart, and it was an obvious approach to try, developing carefully conceived parameterized equations (usually evolved from past projects) that could provide estimation answers. Feed in a bunch of project-specific data, the algorithmists would say, turn the algorithmic crank, and out pop reliable estimates. It didn't work. Study after study (for example, dating back to Mohanty [1981]) showed that, if you took a hypothetical project and fed its data into a collection of proposed algorithmic approaches, those algorithms would produce radically different (by a factor of two to eight) results. Algorithms were no more consistent in the estimates they produced than were those human experts. Subsequent studies have reinforced that depressing finding.

If complex algorithms haven't done the job, some people have reasoned, perhaps simpler algorithmic approaches will. Many people in the field advocate basing an estimate on one or a few key pieces of data—the "lines of code," for example. People say that, if we can predict the number of lines of code (LOC) we expect the system to contain, then we can convert LOC into schedule and cost. (This idea would be laughable—in the sense that it is probably harder to know how many LOC a system will contain than what its schedule and cost will be—if it were not for the fact that so many otherwise bright computer scientists advocate it.) The "function point" (FP). People say that we should look at key parameters such as the number of inputs to and outputs from a system, and base the estimate on that. There is a problem with the FP approach, as well—in fact, there are a couple of problems. The first is that experts disagree on what should be counted and how the counting should happen. The second is that for some applications FPs may make sense, but for others—where, for example, the number of inputs and outputs is far less significant than the complexity of the logic inside the program—FPs make no sense at all. (Some experts supplement FPs with "feature points" for those applications where "functions" are obviously insufficient. But that begs the question, which no one seems to have answered, how many kinds of applications requiring how many kinds of "points" counting schemes are there?)

The bottom line is that, here in the first decade of the twenty-first century, we don't know what constitutes a good estimation approach, one that can yield decent estimates with good confidence that they will really predict when a project will be completed and how much it will cost. That is a discouraging bottom line. Amidst all the clamor to avoid crunch mode and end death marches, it suggests that so long as faulty schedule and cost estimates are the chief management control factors on software projects, we will not see much improvement.

It is important to note that runaway projects, at least those that stem from poor estimation, do not usually occur because the programmers did a poor job of programming. Those projects became runaways because the estimation targets to which they were being managed were largely unreal to begin with. We will explore that factor in several of the facts that follow.

Controversy

There is little controversy about the fact that software estimates are poor. There is lots of controversy as to how better estimation might be done, however. Advocates of algorithmic approaches, for example, tend to support their own algorithms and disparage those of others. Advocates of FP approaches often say terrible things about those who advocate LOC approaches. Jones (1994) lists LOC estimation as responsible for two of the worst "diseases" of the software profession, going so far as to call its use "management malpractice."

There is, happily, some resolution to this controversy, if not to the problem of estimation accuracy. Most students of estimation approaches are beginning to conclude that a "belt and suspenders" approach is the best compromise in the face of this huge problem. They say that an estimate should consist of (a) the opinion of an expert who knows the problem area, plus (b) the output of an algorithm that has been shown, in the past and in this setting, to produce reasonably accurate answers. Those two estimates can then be used to bound the estimation space for the project in question. Those estimates are very unlikely to agree with each other, but some understanding of the envelope of an estimate is better than none at all.

Some recent research findings suggest that "human-mediated estimation process can result in quite accurate estimates," far better than "simple algorithmic models" (Kitchenham et al. 2002). That's a strong vote for expert approaches. It will be worth watching to see if those findings can be replicated.

Sources

There are several studies that have concluded that estimation is one of the top two causes of runaway projects. The following two are examples, as are the three sources listed in the References section that follows.

➡ Cole, Andy. 1995. "Runaway Projects—Causes and Effects." *Software World (UK)* 26, no. 3. This is the best objective study of runaway projects, their causes, their effects, and what people did about them. It concludes that "bad planning and estimating" were a prime causative factor in 48 percent of runaway projects.

➡ Van Genuchten, Michiel. 1991. "Why Is Software Late?" *IEEE Transactions on Software Engineering,* June. This study concludes that "optimistic estimation" is the primary cause of late projects, at 51 percent.

There are several books that point out what happens when a project gets in trouble, often from faulty schedule targets.

➡ Boddie, John. 1987. *Crunch Mode.* Englewood Cliffs, NJ: Yourdon Press.

➡ Yourdon, Ed. 1997. *Death March.* Englewood Cliffs, NJ: Prentice Hall.

References

➡ Jones, Caper. 1994. *Assessment and Control of Software Risks.* Englewood Cliffs, NJ: Yourdon Press. This strongly opinioned book cites "inaccurate metrics" using LOC as "the most serious software risk" and includes four other estimation-related risks in its top five, including "excessive schedule pressure" and "inaccurate cost estimating."

➡ Kitchenham, Barbara, Shari Lawrence Pfleeger, Beth McCall, and Suzanne Eagan. 2002. "An Empirical Study of Maintenance and Development Estimation Accuracy." *Journal of Systems and Software,* Sept.

➡ Mohanty, S. N. 1981. "Software Cost Estimation: Present and Future." In *Software Practice and Experience,* Vol. 11, pp. 103–21.

Fact 9	Most software estimates are performed at the beginning of the life cycle. This makes sense until we realize that estimates are obtained before the requirements are defined and thus before the problem is understood. Estimation, therefore, usually occurs at the wrong time.

Discussion

Why is estimation in the software field as bad as it is? We are about to launch a succession of several facts that can more than account for that badness.

This fact is about estimation timing. We usually make our software estimates at the beginning of a project—right at the very beginning. Sounds OK, right? When else would you expect an estimate to be made? Except for one thing. To make a meaningful estimate, you need to know quite a bit about the project in question. At the very least, you need to know what problem you are to solve. But the first phase of the life cycle, the very beginning of the project, is about requirements determination. That is, in the first phase we establish the requirements the solution is to address. Put more succinctly, requirements determination is about figuring out what problem is to be solved. How can you possibly estimate solution time and cost if you don't yet know what problem you are going to be solving?

This situation is so absurd that, as I present this particular fact at various forums around the software world, I ask my audiences if anyone can contradict what I have just said. After all, this must be one of those "surely I'm wrong" things. But to date, no one has. Instead, there is this general head-nodding that indicates understanding and agreement.

Controversy

Oddly, there seems to be no controversy about this particular fact. That is, as I mentioned earlier, there seems to be general agreement that this fact is correct. The practice it describes is absurd. Someone should be crying out to change things. But no one is.

Sources

I suspect that, like urban legends and old wives' tales, the expression of this particular fact cannot be traced to its origins. Here are a couple of places, however, where the "wrong time" problem has been clearly identified:

- In a Q&A segment of an article, Roger Pressman quotes a questioner as saying, "My problem is that delivery dates and budgets are established before we begin a project. The only question my management asks is 'Can we get this project out the door by June 1?' What's the point in doing detailed project estimates when deadlines and budgets are predefined?" (1992).

- In a flyer for an algorithmic estimation tool (SPC 1998), the text presents this all-too-common conversation: "Marketing Manager (MM): 'So how long d'you think this project will take?' You (the project leader): 'About nine months.' MM: 'We plan to ship this product in six months, tops.' You: 'Six months? No way.' MM: 'You don't seem to understand . . . we've already announced its release date.'"

Note, in these quotes, that not only is estimation being done at the wrong time, but we can make a case for it being done by the wrong people. In fact, we will explore that fact next.

References

➥ Pressman, Roger S. 1992. "Software Project Management: Q and A." *American Programmer* (now *Cutter IT Journal*), Dec.

➥ SPC. 1998. Flyer for the tool Estimate Professional. Software Productivity Centre (Canada).

Fact 10	Most software estimates are made either by upper management or by marketing, not by the people who will build the software or their managers. Estimation is, therefore, done by the wrong people.

Discussion

This is the second fact about why software estimation is as bad as it is. This fact is about who does the estimating.

Common sense would suggest that the people who estimate software projects ought to be folks who know something abut building software. Software engineers. Their projects leaders. Their managers. Common sense gets trumped by politics, in this case. Most often, software estimation is done by the people who want the software product. Upper management. Marketing. Customers and users.

Software estimation, in other words, is currently more about wishes than reality. Management or marketing wants the software product to be available in the first quarter of next year. Ergo, that's the schedule to be met. Note that little or no "estimation" is actually taking place under these circumstances. Schedule and cost targets, derived from some invisible process, are simply being imposed.

Let me tell you a story about software estimation. I once worked for a manager in the aerospace industry who was probably as brilliant as any I have ever known. This manager was contracting to have some software built by another aerospace firm. In the negotiations that determined the contract for building the software, he told them when he needed the software, and they told him that they couldn't achieve that date. Guess which date went into the contract? Time passed, and the wished-for date slid by. The software was eventually delivered when the subcontractor said it would be. But the contract date (I suspect that you guessed correctly which date that was) was not achieved, and there were contractual penalties to be paid by the subcontractor.

There are a couple of points to be made in this story. Even very bright upper managers are capable of making very dumb decisions when political pressure is involved. And there is almost always a price to be paid for working toward an unrealistic deadline. That price is most often paid in human terms (reputation, morale, and health, among others), but—as you can see in this story—there is likely a financial price to be paid as well.

Software estimation, this fact tells us, is being done by the wrong people. And there is serious harm being done to the field because of that.

Controversy

This is another fact where controversy is warranted—and all too absent. Nearly everyone seems to agree that this is a fairly normal state of affairs. Whether it should be a desirable state of affairs is an issue that is rarely raised. But this fact does raise a major disconnect between those who know something about software and those who do not. Or perhaps this fact results from such a disconnect that already exists.

Let me explain. The disconnect that results is that software people may not know what *is* possible in estimating a project, but they almost always know what *is not* possible. And when upper management (or marketing) fails to listen to such knowledgeable words of warning, software people tend to lose faith and trust in those who are giving them direction. And they also lose a whole lot of motivation.

On the other hand, there is already a long-standing disconnect between software folks and their upper management A litany of failed expectations has caused upper management to lose its own faith and trust in software folks. When software people say they can't meet a wish list estimate, upper management simply ignores them. After all, what would be the basis on which they might believe them, given that software people so seldom do what they say they will do?

All of this says that the software field has a major disconnect problem (we return to this thought in Fact 13). The controversy, in the case of this particular fact, is less about whether the fact is true and more about why the fact is true. And until that particular controversy gets solved, the software field will continue to be in a great deal of trouble.

 ## Sources

There is actually a research study that explores precisely this issue and demonstrates this fact. In it (Lederer 1990), the author explores the issue of what he calls "political" versus "rational" estimation practices. (The choice of words is fascinating—political estimation is performed, as you might guess, by those upper managers and the marketing folks; rational estimation [I particularly love this choice of words], on the other hand, is performed by the software folk. And in this study, political estimation was the norm.)

In another reported study (CASE 1991), the authors found that most estimates (70 percent) are done by someone associated with the "user department," and the smallest number (4 percent) are done by the "project team." The user department may or may not be the same as upper management or marketing, but it certainly represents estimation by the wrong people.

There have been other similar, studies in other application domains (note that these studies were about Information Systems). The two quotes in the source material for the previous fact, for example, not only are about doing estimation at the wrong time, but are also about the wrong people doing that estimation.

References

➥ CASE. 1991. "CASE/CASM Industry Survey Report." HCS, Inc., P.O. Box 40770, Portland, OR 97240.

➥ Lederer, Albert. 1990. "Information System Cost Estimating." *MIS Quarterly*, June.

Fact 11	Software estimates are rarely adjusted as the project proceeds. Thus those estimates done at the wrong time by the wrong people are usually not corrected.

Discussion

Let's look at common sense again. Given how bad software estimates apparently are, wouldn't you think that, as a project proceeds and everyone learns more about what its likely outcome will be, those early and usually erroneous estimates would be adjusted to meet reality? Common sense strikes out again. Software people tend to have to live or die by those original faulty estimates. Upper management is simply not interested in revising them. Given that they so often represent wishes instead of realistic estimates, why should upper management allow those wishes to be tampered with?

Oh, projects may track how things are progressing and which milestones have to slide and perhaps even where the final milestones should be extended to. But when the time comes to total a project's results, its failure or success is usually measured by those first-out-of-the-box numbers. You remember, the numbers concocted at the wrong time by the wrong people?

Controversy

This failure to revisit early estimates is obviously bad practice. But few fight against this in any concerted way. (There was, however, one study [NASA 1990] that advocated reestimation and even defined the points in the life cycle at which it ought to occur. But I am not aware of anyone following this advice.) Thus, although there should be enormous controversy about this particular fact, I know of none. Software folks simply accept as a given that they will not be allowed to revise the estimates under which they are working.

Of course, once a project has careened past its original estimation date, there is public hue and cry about when product is likely to become available. The baggage handling system at the Denver International Airport comes to mind. So does each new delivery of a Microsoft product. So there is controversy about the relationship between political estimates and real outcomes. But almost always, that controversy focuses on blaming the software folks. Once again, "blame the victim" wins, and common sense loses.

 ## Sources

I know of no research study on this issue. There are plenty of anecdotes about failure to reestimate, however, in both the popular computing press and software management books. I rely on these things to substantiate this fact:

1. Examples such as those mentioned earlier (the Denver Airport and Microsoft products)

2. My own 40-something years of experience in the software field

3. The half-dozen books I've written on studies of failed software projects

4. The fact that when I present this fact in public forums and invite the audience to disagree with me ("please tell me that I'm wrong"), no one does

 ## Reference

➡ NASA. 1990. *Manager's Handbook for Software Development.* NASA-Goddard.

Fact 12   Since estimates are so faulty, there is little reason to be concerned when software projects do not meet estimated targets. But everyone is concerned anyway.

Discussion

Last chance, common sense. Given how bad software estimates are—that wrong time, wrong people, no change phenomenon we've just discussed—you'd think that estimates would be treated as relatively unimportant. Right? Wrong! In fact software projects are almost always managed by schedule. Because of that, schedule is considered—by upper management, at least—as the most important factor in software.

Let me be specific. Management by schedule means establishing a bunch of short-term and long-term milestones (the tiny ones are sometimes called inch-pebbles) and deciding whether the project is succeeding or failing by what happens at those schedule points. You're behind schedule at milestone 26? Your project is in trouble.

How else could we manage software projects? Let me give just a few examples to show that management by schedule isn't the only way of doing business.

- We could manage by product. We could proclaim success or failure by how much of the final product is available and working.

- We could manage by issue. We could proclaim success or failure by how well and how rapidly we are resolving those issues that always arise during the course of a project.

- We could manage by risk. We could proclaim success or failure by a succession of demonstrations that the risks identified at the beginning of the project have been overcome.

- We could manage by business objectives. We could proclaim success or failure by how well the software improves business performance.

- We could even manage (gasp!) by quality. We could proclaim success or failure by how many quality attributes the product has successfully achieved.

"How naive this guy is," I can hear you muttering under your breath, thinking about what I have just finished saying here. "In this fast-paced age, schedule really does matter more than anything else." Well, perhaps. But isn't there something wrong with managing to estimates, the least controllable, least correct, most questionable factor that managers handle?

Controversy

Everyone, software people included, simply accept that management by schedule is the way we do things. There is plenty of resentment of the aftereffects of management by schedule, but no one seems to be stepping up to the plate to do something about it.

Some new ideas on this subject may shake this status quo, however. Extreme Programming (Beck 2000) suggests that after the customer or user chooses three of the four factors—cost, schedule, features, and quality—the software developers get to choose the fourth. This nicely identifies the things at stake on a software project, and we can see clearly that only two of them are about estimates. It also proposes to change the power structure that is currently such a major contributor to poor estimation.

Source

I know of no research on this matter. But in software workshops I have conducted little experiments that tend to illustrate this problem. Let me describe one of those experiments.

I ask the attendees to work on a small task. I deliberately give them too much to do and not enough time to do it. My expectation is that the attendees will try to do the whole job, do it correctly, and therefore will produce an unfinished product because they run out of time. Not so. To a person, these attendees scramble mightily to achieve my impossible schedule. They produce sketchy and shoddy products that appear to be complete but cannot possibly work.

What does that tell me? That, in our culture today, people are trying so hard to achieve (impossible) schedules that they are willing to sacrifice completeness and quality in getting there. That there has been a successful conditioning process, one that has resulted in people doing the wrong things for the wrong reasons. And finally, and most disturbingly, that it will be very difficult to turn all of this around.

Extreme Programming is best described by the source listed in the Reference section to follow.

Reference

➥ Beck, Kent. 2000. *eXtreme Programming Explained.* Boston: Addison-Wesley.

| **Fact 13** | There is a disconnect between management and their programmers. In one research study of a project that failed to meet its estimates and was seen by its management as a failure, the technical participants saw it as the most successful project they had ever worked on. |

 ## Discussion

You could see this one coming. With all the estimation problems discussed earlier, it is hardly surprising that many technologists are trying very hard to pay no attention to estimates and deadlines. They don't always succeed, as I pointed out in my workshop experiment described in Fact 12. But it is tempting to those who understand how unreal most of our estimates are to use some factor other than estimation to judge the success of their project.

One research study doth not a groundswell make. But this particular study is so impressive and so important, I couldn't help but include it here as a possible future fact, an indicator of what may begin to happen more often.

This discussion focuses on a research project described in Linberg (1999). Linberg studied a particular real-world software project, one that management had called a failure, and one that had careened madly past its estimation targets. He asked the technologists on the project to talk about the most successful project they had ever worked on. The plot thickens! Those technologists, or at least five out of eight of them, identified this most recent project as their most successful. Management's failed project was a great success, according to its participants. What a bizarre illustration of the disconnect we have been discussing!

What on earth was this project about? Here are some of the project facts. It was 419 percent over budget. It was over schedule by 193 percent (27 months versus the estimate of 14). It was over its original size estimates by 130 percent for its software and 800 percent for its firmware. But the project was successfully completed. It did what it was supposed to do (control a medical instrument). It fulfilled its requirement of "no postrelease software defects."

So there are the seeds of a disconnect. Estimated targets didn't even come close to being achieved. But the software product, once it was available, did what it was supposed to do and did it well.

Still, doesn't it seem unlikely that putting a working, useful product on the air would make this a "most successful" project? Wouldn't that be an experience you would have hoped these technologists had had many times before? The answer to those questions, for the study in question, was the expected "yes." There was

something else that caused the technologists to see this project as a success—
several something elses, in fact.

- The product worked the way it was supposed to work (no surprise there).
- Developing the product had been a technical challenge. (Lots of data show that, most of all, technologists really like overcoming a tough problem.)
- The team was small and high performing.
- Management was "the best I've ever worked with." Why? "Because the team was given the freedom to develop a good design," because there was no "scope creep," and because "I never felt pressure from the schedule."

And the participants added something else. Linberg asked them for their perceptions about why the project was late. They said this:

- The schedule estimates were unrealistic (ta-da!).
- There was a lack of resources, particularly expert advice.
- Scope was poorly understood at the outset.
- The project started late.

There is something particularly fascinating about these perceptions. All of them are about things that were true at the beginning of the project. Not along the way, but *at the beginning*. In other words, the die was cast on this project from day one. No matter how well and how hard those technologists had worked, they were unlikely to have satisfied management's expectations. Given that, they did what, from their point of view, was the next best thing. They had a good time producing a useful product.

There have been other studies of management and technologist perceptions that also reflect a major disconnect. For example, in one (Colter and Cougar 1983), managers and technologists were asked about some characteristics of software maintenance. Managers believed that changes were typically large, involving more than 200 LOC. Technologists reported that changes actually involved only 50 to 100 LOC. Managers believed that the number of changed LOC correlated with the time to do the task; technologists said that there was no such correlation.

And on the subject of software runaways, there is evidence that technologists see the problem coming far before their management does (72 percent of the time) (Cole 1995). The implication is that what the technologists see coming is not passed on to management—the ultimate disconnect.

Perhaps the most fascinating comments on this subject came from a couple of articles on project management. Jeffery and Lawrence (1985) found that "projects where no estimates were prepared at all fared best on productivity" (versus projects where estimates were performed by technologists [next best] or their managers [worst]). Landsbaum and Glass (1992) found "a very strong correlation between level of productivity and a feeling of control" (that is, when the programmers felt in control of their fate, they were much more productive). In other words, control-focused management does not necessarily lead to the best project or even to the most productive one.

Controversy

There are essentially two aspects to this fact: the problem of what constitutes project success and the problem of a disconnect between management and technologists.

With respect to the "success" issue, the Linberg research finding has not been replicated as of this writing, so there has been no time for controversy to have emerged about this fact. My suspicion is that management, upon reading this story and reflecting on this fact, would in general be horrified that a project so "obviously" a failure could be seen as a success by these technologists. My further suspicion is that most technologists, upon reading this story and reflecting on this fact, would find it all quite reasonable. If my suspicions are correct, there is essentially an unspoken controversy surrounding the issue this fact addresses. And that controversy is about what constitutes project success. If we can't agree on a definition of a successful project, then the field has some larger problems that need sorting out. My suspicion is that you haven't by any means heard the last of this particular fact and issue.

With regard to the disconnect issue, I have seen almost nothing commenting on it in the literature. Quotes like the ones from Jeffery and Landsbaum seem to be treated like the traditional griping of those at the bottom of a management hierarchy toward those above them, rather than information that may have real significance.

Sources

Another relevant source, in addition to those in the References section, is

➥ Procaccino, J. Drew, and J. M. Verner. 2001. "Practitioner's Perceptions of Project Success: A Pilot Study." *IEEE International Journal of Computer and Engineering Management.*

References

➥ Cole, Andy. 1995. "Runaway Projects—Causes and Effects." *Software World (UK)* 26, no. 3.

➥ Colter, Mel, and Dan Couger. 1983. From a study reported in *Software Maintenance Workshop Record.* Dec. 6.

➥ Jeffery, D. R., and M. J. Lawrence. 1985. "Managing Programmer Productivity." *Journal of Systems and Software,* Jan.

➥ Landsbaum, Jerome B., and Robert L. Glass. 1992. *Measuring and Motivating Maintenance Programmers.* Englewood Cliffs, NJ: Prentice-Hall.

➥ Linberg, K. R. 1999. "Software Developer Perceptions about Software Project Failure: A Case Study." *Journal of Systems and Software* 49, nos. 2/3, Dec. 30.

Fact 14   The answer to a feasibility study is almost always "yes."

Discussion

The "new kid on the block" phenomenon affects the software field in a lot of different ways. One of the ways is that we "don't get no respect." There is the feeling among traditionalists in the disciplines whose problems we solve that they have gotten along without software for many decades, thank you very much, and they can get along without us just fine now.

That played out in a "theater of the absurd" event some years ago when an engineering manager on a pilotless aircraft project took that point of view. It didn't matter that a pilotless aircraft simply couldn't function at all without computers and software. This guy wanted to dump all of that troublesome technology overboard and get on with his project.

Another way the "new kid on the block" phenomenon hits us is that we seem to possess all-too-often incurable optimism. It's as if, since no one has ever been able to solve the problems we are able to solve, we believe that no new problem is too tough for us to solve. And, astonishingly often, that is true. But there are times when it's not, times when that optimism gets us in a world of trouble. When we believe that we can finish this project by tomorrow, or at least by a couple of tomorrows from now. When we believe we will instantly produce software without errors and then find that the error-removal phase often takes more time than systems analysis, design, and coding put together.

And then there is the feasibility study. This optimism really gets us in trouble when technical feasibility is an issue. The result is, for those (all-too-few) projects when a feasibility study precedes the actual system construction project, the answer to the feasibility study is almost invariably "yes, we can do that." And, for a certain percentage of the time, that turns out to be the wrong answer. But we don't find *that* out until many months later.

Controversy

There is such a time gap between getting the wrong answer to a feasibility study and the discovery that it really was the wrong answer, that we rarely connect those two events. Because of that, there is less controversy about this fact than you would tend to expect. Probably the existence of a feasibility study (they are all-too-seldom performed) is more controversial than the fact that they all too often give the wrong answer.

Source

The source for this fact is particularly interesting to me. I was attending the International Conference on Software Engineering (ICSE) in Tokyo in 1987, and the famed Jerry Weinberg was the keynote speaker. As part of his presentation, he asked the audience how many of them had ever participated in a feasibility study where the answer came back "No." There was uneasy silence in the audience, then laughter. Not a single hand rose. All 1,500 or so of us realized at the same time, I think, that Jerry's question touched on an important phenomenon in the field, one we had simply never thought about before.

REUSE

Fact 15	Reuse-in-the-small (libraries of subroutines) began nearly 50 years ago and is a well-solved problem.

Discussion

There is a tendency in the computing world to assume that any good idea that comes along must be a new idea. Case in point—reuse.

Truth to tell, the notion of reuse is as old as the software field. In the mid-1950s, a user organization for scientific applications of IBM "mainframes" (that term was not used in those days) was formed. One of its most important functions was serving as a clearinghouse for contributed software subroutines. The organization was called Share, appropriately enough, and the contributed routines became the first library of reusable software. The way to gain fame, back in those early computing days, was to be known as someone who contributed good quality routines to the library. (It was not, however, a way of gaining fortune. Back in those days, software had no monetary value—it was given away free with hardware. Note, here, another good idea that is not new—open-source or freeware software.)

Now those early libraries of software routines contained what we today would call reuse-in-the-small routines. Math functions. Sorts and merges. Limited-scope debuggers. Character string handlers. All those wonderful housekeeping capabilities that most programmers needed (and still need) at one time or another. In fact, my first brush with (extremely limited!) fame came in contributing a debug routine addendum to the Share library.

Reuse was built into the software development process, back in those days. If you were writing a program that needed some kind of common capability, you went first to the Share library to see if it already existed. (Other user groups, like Guide and Common, probably had their own libraries for their own application domains. I was not a business application programmer at that time, so I don't really know whether Guide and Common functioned like Share.) I remember writing a program that needed a random number generator and going to the Share library to find one I could use. (There were plenty of them, from your basic random number generator to those that generated random numbers to some predictable pattern, like fitting a normal curve.)

Reuse in those days was catch-as-catch-can, with no quality control on what was placed in the library. However, having your name attached to a Share library routine was a big deal, and you worked very hard to make sure your contribution was error-free before you submitted it. I don't remember any quality problems with reused Share routines.

Why this trip down memory lane? Because it is important in trying to understand the reuse phenomenon and its status today, to realize that this is a very old and very successful idea. Following the success of reuse-in-the-small, and, in spite of efforts to expand that concept into larger components, the state of reuse remained fairly constant over the years. Why that is will be discussed in Fact 16.

Controversy

The primary controversy here is that too many people in the computing field think that reuse is a brand-new idea. As a result, there is enormous (and often hyped) enthusiasm for this concept, an enthusiasm that would be more realistic if people understood its history and its failure to grow over the years.

Sources

This memory of early days' reuse is very vivid for me. In fact, the best account of this phenomenon is in my own personal/professional reflection (Glass 1998) (he immodestly said). The Share organization (it still functions today) would be another place to find documentation of its early days (it actually produced what we would today call a tools and parts catalog, wherein potential users could find out what modules were available to them, organized by the problem those modules solved).

Reference

➥ Glass, Robert L. 1998. "Software Reflections—A Pioneer's View of the History of the Field." In *In the Beginning: Personal Recollections of Software Pioneers.* Los Alamitos, CA: IEEE Computer Society Press.

Fact 16	**Reuse-in-the-large (components) remains a mostly unsolved problem, even though everyone agrees it is important and desirable.**

Discussion

It is one thing to build useful small software components. It is quite another to build useful large ones. In Fact 15, we solved the reuse-in-the-small problem as far back as more than 40-something years ago. But the reuse-in-the-large problem has remained unsolved over those same intervening years.

Why is that? Because there are a lot of different opinions on this subject, I address this "why" question in the Controversy section that follows.

But the key word in understanding this problem is the word *useful.* It is not very difficult to build generalized, reusable routines. Oh, it is more difficult—some say three times more difficult than it is to build comparable special-purpose routines (there's a fact, Fact 18, that covers this)—but that is not a prohibitive barrier. The problem is, once those reusable modules are built, they have to do something that truly matches a great variety of needs in a great variety of programs.

And there's the rub. We see in the discussion of the controversy surrounding this topic that (according to one collection of viewpoints, at least) a diverse collection of problems to be solved results in a diverse set of component needs—too diverse, at least at this time, to make reuse-in-the-large viable.

Controversy

There is considerable controversy surrounding the topic of reuse-in-the-large. First, advocates see reuse-in-the-large as the future of the field, a future in which programs are screwed together from existing components (they call it component-based software engineering). Others, typically practitioners who understand the field better (there's no bias in that comment!), pooh-pooh the idea. They say that it is nearly impossible to generalize enough functions to allow finessing the development of special-purpose, fitted to the problem at hand, components.

The resolution of this particular controversy falls into a topic that might be called software diversity. If there are enough common problems across projects and even application domains, then component-based approaches will eventually prevail. If, as many suspect, the diversity of applications and domains means that no two problems are very similar to one another, then only those common housekeeping functions and tasks are likely to be generalized, and they constitute only a small percentage of a typical program's code.

There is one source of data to shed light on this matter. NASA-Goddard, which over the years has studied software phenomena at its Software Engineering Laboratory (SEL) and which services the very limited application domain of flight dynamics software, has found that up to 70 percent of its programs can be built from reused modules. Even the SEL, however, sees that fact as a function of having a tightly constrained application domain and does not anticipate achieving that level of success across more diverse tasks.

Second, there is a controversy in the field as to why reuse-in-the-large has never caught on. Many, especially academics, believe it is because practitioners are stubborn, applying the "not-invented-here" (NIH) syndrome to allow them to ignore the work of others. Most people who believe in NIH tend to view management as the problem—and the eventual solution. From that point of view, the problems of reuse-in-the-large are about will, not skill. It is management's task, these people say, to establish policies and procedures that foster reuse to create the necessary will.

In fact, few claim that there is a problem of skill in reuse. Although it is generally acknowledged that it is considerably more difficult to built a generalized, reusable version of a capability than its ad hoc alternative, it is also generally acknowledged that there is no problem in finding people able to do that job.

My own view, which contradicts both the NIH view and the will-not-skill view, is that the problem is close to being intractable. That is, because of the diversity problem mentioned earlier, it is the exception rather than the rule to find a component that would be truly generalizable across a multiplicity of applications, let alone domains. My reason for holding that view is that over the years one of the tasks I set for myself was to evolve reuse-in-the-small into reuse-in-the-large. I sought and tried to build reuse-in-the-large components that would have all the widespread usefulness of those reuse-in-the-small routines from the Share library. And I came to understand, as few today seem to understand, how difficult a task that really is. For example, knowing that one of the bread-and-butter tools in the Information Systems application domain was the generalized report generator, I tried to produce the analogous capability for the scientific/engineering domain. Despite months of struggle, I could never find enough commonality in the scientific/engineering report generation needs to define the requirements for such a component, let alone build one.

In my view, then, the failure of reuse-in-the-large is likely to continue. It is not an NIH problem. It is not a will problem. It is not even a skill problem. It is simply a problem too hard to be solved, one rooted in software diversity.

No one wants me to be correct, of course. Certainly, I don't. Screwed-together components would be a wonderful way to build software. So would automatic generation of code from a requirements specification. And neither of those, in my view, is ever likely to happen in any meaningful way.

 ## Sources

There are plenty of sources of material on reuse-in-the-large, but almost all of them present the viewpoint that it is a solvable problem.

As mentioned earlier, one subset of this Pollyanna viewpoint consists of those who see it as a management problem and present approaches that management can use to create the necessary will. Two recent sources of this viewpoint are

➥ IEEE Standard 1517. "Standard for Information Technology—Software Life Cycle Processes—Reuse Processes; 1999." A standard, produced by the engineering society IEEE, by means of which the construction of reusable componentry can be fostered

➥ McClure, Carma. 2001. *Software Reuse—A Standards-Based Guide.* Los Alamitos, CA: IEEE Computer Society Press. A how-to book for applying the IEEE standard.

Over the years, a few authors have been particularly realistic in their view of reuse. Any of the writings of Ted Biggerstaff, Will Tracz, and Don Reifer on this subject are worth reading.

➥ Reifer, Donald J. 1997. *Practical Software Reuse.* New York: John Wiley and Sons.

➥ Tracz, Will. 1995. *Confessions of a Used Program Salesman: Institutionalizing Reuse.* Reading, MA: Addison-Wesley.

Fact 17	**Reuse-in-the-large works best in families of related systems and thus is domain-dependent. This narrows the potential applicability of reuse-in-the-large.**

 ### Discussion

OK, so reuse-in-the-large is a difficult, if not intractable, problem. Is there any way in which we can increase the odds of making it work?

The answer is "yes." It may be nearly impossible to find components of consequence that can be reused across application domains, but within a domain, the picture improves dramatically. The SEL experience in building software for the flight dynamics domain is a particularly encouraging example.

Software people speak of "families" of applications and "product lines" and "family-specific architectures." Those are the people who are realistic enough to believe that reuse-in-the-large, if it is ever to succeed, must be done in a collection of programs that attacks the same kinds of problems. Payroll programs, perhaps even human resource programs. Data reduction programs for radar data. Inventory control programs. Trajectory programs for space missions. Notice the number of adjectives that it takes to specify a meaningful domain, one for which reuse-in-the-large might work.

Reuse-in-the-large, when applied to a narrowly defined application domain, has a good chance of being successful. Cross-project and cross-domain reuse, on the other hand, does not (McBreen 2002).

Controversy

The controversy surrounding this particular fact is among people who don't want to give up on the notion of fully generalized reuse-in-the-large. Some of those people are vendors selling reuse-in-the-large support products. Others are academics who understand very little about application domains and want to believe that domain-specific approaches aren't necessary. There is a philosophical connection between these latter people and the one-size-fits-all tools and methodologists. They would like to believe that the construction of software is the same no matter what domain is being addressed. And they are wrong.

Sources

The genre of books on software product families and product architectures is growing rapidly. This is, in another words, a fact that many are just beginning to grasp, and a bandwagon of supporters of the fact is now being established. A couple of very recent books that address this topic in a domain-focused way are

➡ Bosch, Jan. 2000. *Design and Use of Software Architectures: Adopting and Evolving a Product-Line Approach.* Boston: Addison-Wesley.

➡ Jazayeri, Mehdi, Alexander Ran, and Frank van der Linden. 2000. *Software Architecture for Product Families: Principles and Practice.* Boston: Addison-Wesley.

Reference

➡ McBreen, Pete. 2002. *Software Craftsmanship.* Boston: Addison-Wesley. Says "cross-project reuse is very hard to achieve."

Fact 18	There are two "rules of three" in reuse: (a) It is three times as difficult to build reusable components as single use components, and (b) a reusable component should be tried out in three different applications before it will be sufficiently general to accept into a reuse library.

Discussion

There is nothing magic about the number three in reuse circles. In the two rules of three, those threes are rules of thumb, nothing more. But they are nice, memorable, realistic rules of thumb.

The first is about the effort needed to build reusable components. As we have seen, to construct reusable components is a complex task. Often, someone building a reusable component is thinking of a particular problem to be solved and trying to determine whether there is some more general problem analogous to this specific one. A reusable component, of course, must solve this more general problem in such a way that it solves the specific one as well.

Not only must the component itself be generalized, but the testing approach for the component must address the generalized problem. Thus the complexity of building a reusable component arises in the requirements—"what is the generalized problem?"—design, "how can I solve this generalized problem? in coding, and in testing portions of the life cycle. In other words, from start to finish.

It is no wonder that knowledgeable reuse experts say it takes three times as long. It is also worth pointing out that, although most people are capable of thinking about problems in a generalized way, it still requires a different mindset from simply solving the problem at hand. Many advocate the use of particularly skilled, expert generalizers.

The second rule of thumb is about being sure that your reusable component really is generalized. It is not enough to show that it solves your problem at hand. It must solve some related problems, problems that may not have been so clearly in mind when the component was being developed. Once again, the number three—try your component out in three different settings—is arbitrary. My guess is that it represents a minimum constraint. That is, I would recommend trying out your generalized component in *at least* three different applications before concluding that it truly is generalized.

Controversy

This fact represents a couple of rules of thumb, rules that few have reason to doubt. Everyone would acknowledge that reusable components are harder to develop and require more verification than their single-task brethren. The numbers three might be argued by some, but there is hardly anyone who is likely to defend them to the death, since they are rules of thumb and nothing more.

Sources

This fact has come to be known over the years as "Biggerstaff's Rules of Three." There is a very early paper by Ted Biggerstaff, published in the 1960s or 1970s, that first mentions reuse rules of three. Unfortunately, the passage of time has eroded by ability to recall the specific reference, and my many attempts to use the Internet to overcome that memory loss have not helped. However, in the References section, I mention studies of Biggerstaff's role.

I have a particular reason for remembering the rules of thumb and Biggerstaff, however. At the time Biggerstaff's material was published, I was working on a generalized report generator program for business applications (I mentioned it earlier in passing). I had been given three report generators (for very specific tasks) to program, and—since I had never written a report generator program before—I gave more than the usual amount of thought to the problem.

The development of the first of the three generators went quite slowly, as I thought about all the problems that, to me, were unique. Summing up columns of figures. Summing sums. Summing sums of sums. There were some interesting problems, very different from the scientific domain that I was accustomed to, to be solved here.

The second program didn't go much faster. The reason was that I was beginning to realize how much these three programs were going to have in common, and it had occurred to me that a generalized solution might even work.

The third program went quite smoothly. The generalized approaches that had evolved in addressing the second problem (while remembering the first) worked nicely. Not only was the result of the third programming effort the third required report generator, but it also resulted in a general-purpose report generator. (I called it JARGON. The origin of the acronym is embarrassing and slightly complicated, but forgive me while I explain it. The company for which I worked at the time was Aerojet. The homegrown operating system we used there was called Nimble. And JARGON stood for Jeneralized (ouch!) Aerojet Report Generator on Nimble.)

Now, I had already formed the opinion that thinking through all three specific projects had been necessary to evolve the generalized solution. In fact, I had formed the opinion that the only reasonable way to create a generalized problem solution was to create three solutions to specific versions of that problem. And along came Biggerstaff's paper. You can see why I have remembered it all these years.

Unfortunately, I can't verify the first rule of three, the one about it taking three times as long. But I am absolutely certain that, in creating JARGON, it took me considerably longer than producing one very specific report generator. I find the number three quite credible in this context, also.

➡ Biggerstaff, Ted, and Alan J. Perlis, eds. 1989. *Software Reusability.* New York: ACM Press.

➡ Tracz, Will. 1995. *Confessions of a Used Program Salesman: Institutionalizing Reuse.* Reading, MA: Addison-Wesley.

> **Fact 19** — Modification of reused code is particularly error-prone. If more than 20 to 25 percent of a component is to be revised, it is more efficient and effective to rewrite it from scratch.

Discussion

So reuse-in-the-large is very difficult (if not impossible), except for families of applications, primarily because of the diversity of the problems solved by software. So why not just change the notion of reuse-in-the-large a little bit? Instead of reusing components as is, why not modify them to fit the problem at hand? Then, with appropriate modifications, we could get those components to work anywhere, even in totally unrelated families of applications.

As it turns out, that idea is a dead end also. Because of the complexity involved in building and maintaining significant software systems (we will return to this concept in future facts), modifying existing software can be quite difficult. Typically, a software system is built to a certain design envelope (the framework that enables but at the same time bounds the chosen solution) and with a design philosophy (different people will often choose very different approaches to building the same software solution). Unless the person trying to modify a piece of software understands that envelope and accepts that philosophy, it will be very difficult to complete a modification successfully.

Furthermore, often a design envelope fits the problem at hand very nicely but may completely constrain solving any problem not accommodated within the envelope, such as the one required to make a component reusable across domains. (Note that this is a problem inherent in the Extreme Programming approach, which opts for early and simple design solutions, making subsequent modification to fit an enhancement to the original solution potentially very difficult.)

There is another problem underlying the difficulties of modifying existing software. Those who have studied the tasks of software maintenance find that there is one task whose difficulties overwhelm all the other tasks of modifying software. That task is "comprehending the existing solution." It is a well-known phenomenon in software that even the programmer who originally built the solution may find it difficult to modify some months later.

To solve those problems, software people have invented the notion of maintenance documentation— documentation that describes how a program works and why it works that way. Often such documentation starts with the original software design document and builds on that. But here we run into another software phenomenon. Although everyone accepts the need for maintenance documentation, its creation is usually the first piece of baggage thrown overboard when a software project gets in cost or schedule trouble. As a result, the number of software systems with adequate maintenance documentation is nearly nil.

To make matters worse, during maintenance itself, as the software is modified (and modification is the dominant activity of the software field, as we see in Fact 42), whatever maintenance documentation exists is probably not modified to match. The result is that there may or may not be any maintenance documentation, but if there is, it is quite likely out-of-date and therefore unreliable. Given all of that, most software maintenance is done from reading the code.

And there we are back to square one. It is difficult to modify software. Things that might help are seldom employed or are employed improperly. And the reason for the lack of such support is often our old enemies, schedule and cost pressure. There is a Catch-22 here, and until we find another way of managing software projects, this collection of dilemmas is unlikely to change.

There is a corollary to this particular fact about revising software components:

It is almost always a mistake to modify packaged, vendor-produced software systems.

It is a mistake because such modification is quite difficult; that's what we have just finished discussing. But it is a mistake for another reason. With vendor-supplied software, there are typically rereleases of the product, wherein the vendor solves old problems, adds new functionality, or both. Usually, it is desirable for customers to employ such new releases (in fact, vendors often stop maintaining old releases after some period of time, at which point users may have no choice but to upgrade to a new release).

The problem with in-house package modifications is that they must be redone with every such new release. And if the vendor changes the solution approach sufficiently, the old modification may have to be redesigned totally to fit into the new version. Thus modifying packaged software is a never-ending proposition, one that continues to cost each time a new version is used. In addition to the unpleasant financial costs of doing that, there is probably no task that software people hate more than making the same old modification to a piece of software over and over again. Morale costs join dollar costs as the primary reason for accepting this corollary as fact.

There is nothing new about this corollary. I can remember back to the 1960s when, considering how to solve a particular problem, rejecting modifying vendor software on the grounds that it would be, long-term, the most disastrous solution approach. Unfortunately, as with many of the other frequently forgotten facts discussed in this book, we seem to have to keep learning that lesson over and over again.

In some research I did on the maintenance of Enterprise Resource Planning (ERP) systems (for example, SAPs), several users said that they had modified the ERP software in-house, only to back out of those changes when they realized to their horror what they had signed up for.

Note that this same problem has interesting ramifications for the open-source software movement. It is easy to access open-source code to modify it, but the wisdom of doing so is clearly questionable, unless the once-modified version of the open-source code is to become a new fork in the system's development, never to merge with the standard version again. I have never heard open-source advocates discuss this particular problem. (One solution, of course, would be for the key players for the open-source code in question to accept those in-house modifications as part of the standard version. But there is never any guarantee that they will choose to do that.)

Controversy

To accept these facts, it is necessary to accept another fact—that software products are difficult to build and maintain. Software practitioners generally accept this notion. There is, unfortunately, a belief (typically among those who have never built production-quality software) that constructing and maintaining software solutions is easy. Often this belief emerges from those who have never seen the software solution to a problem of any magnitude, either because they have dealt only with toy problems (this is a problem for many academics and their students) or because their only exposure to software has been through some sort of computer literacy course wherein the most complicated piece of software examined was one that displayed "Hello, World" on a screen.

Because of the rampant naïveté inherent in that belief, there are many who simply will not accept the fact that modifying existing software is difficult. Those people, therefore, will continue to hold the belief that solution modification is the right approach to overcoming the diversity problems of reuse-in-the-large (and, I suppose, for tailoring vendor packages). There is probably nothing to be done for people who adhere to that belief—except to ignore them whenever possible.

 ## Sources

The primary fact here was discovered in research studies of software errors and software cost estimation. The SEL of NASA-Goddard—an organization that we discuss frequently in this book—conducted studies of precisely the problem of whether modifying old code was more cost-effective than starting a new version from scratch (McGarry et al. 1984; Thomas 1997). Their findings were impressive and quite clear. If a software system is to be modified at or above the 20 to 25 percent level, then it is cheaper and easier to start over and build a new product. That percentage is low—surprisingly low, in fact.

You may recall that the SEL specializes in software for a very specific application domain—flight dynamics. You may also recall that the SEL has been extremely successful in using reuse-in-the-large to solve problems in their very specialized domain. One might choose to question his or her findings on the grounds that they might differ for other domains; but, on the other hand, my tendency is to accept them because (a) the SEL appears to be more than objective in its explorations of this (and other) subjects, (b) SEL was quite motivated to make reuse-in-the-large work in whatever way it could be made to work, and (c) my own experience is that modifying software built by someone else is extremely difficult to get right. (Not to mention that famous quotation from Fred Brooks [1995], "software work is the most complex that humanity has ever undertaken."

References

➤ Brooks, Frederick P., Jr. 1995. *The Mythical Man-Month.* Anniversary ed. Reading, MA: Addison Wesley.

➤ McGarry, F., G. Page, D. Card, et al. 1984. "An Approach to Software Cost Estimation." NASA Software Engineering Laboratory, SEL-83-001 (Feb.). This study found the figure to be 20 percent.

➤ Thomas, William, Alex Delis, and Victor R. Basili. 1997. "An Analysis of Errors in a Reuse-Oriented Development Environment." *Journal of Systems and Software* 38, no. 3. This study reports the 25 percent figure.

Fact 20	Design pattern reuse is one solution to the problems inherent in code reuse.

Discussion

Up until now, this discussion of reuse has been pretty discouraging. Reuse-in-the-small is a well-solved problem and has been for over 45 years. Reuse-in-the-large is a nearly intractable problem, one we may never solve except within application families of similar problems. And modifying reusable components is often difficult and not a very good idea. So what's a programmer to do to avoid starting from scratch on each new problem that comes down the pike?

One thing that software practitioners have always done is to solve today's problem by remembering yesterday's solution. They used to carry code listings from one job to the next, until the time came that software had value (in the 1970s), and then various corporate contractual provisions and some laws made it illegal to do.

One way or another, of course, programmers still do. They may carry their prior solutions in their heads or they may actually carry them on disk or paper, but the need to reuse yesterday's solution in today's program is too compelling to quit doing it entirely. As a legal consultant, I have, on occasion, been called on to deal with the consequences of such occurrences.

Those transported solutions are often not reinstated verbatim from the old code. More often, those previous solutions are kept because of the design concepts that are embodied in the code. At a conference a couple of decades ago, Visser (1987) reported what most practitioners already know: "Designers rarely start from scratch."

What we are saying here is that there is another level at which to talk about reuse. We can talk about reusing code, as we have just finished doing. And we can talk about reusing design. Design reuse exploded dramatically in the 1990s. It was an idea as old as software itself; and yet, when it was packaged in the new form of "design patterns," suddenly it had new applicability—and new respect. Design patterns, nicely defined and discussed in the first book on the subject (Gamma 1995), gained immediate credibility in both the practitioner and academic communities.

What is a design pattern? It is a description of a problem that occurs over and over again, accompanied by a design solution to that problem. A pattern has four essential elements: a name, a description of when the solution should be applied, the solution itself, and the consequences of using that solution.

Why were patterns so quickly accepted by the field? Practitioners recognized that what was happening here was something they had always done, but now it was cloaked in new structure and new respectability. Academics recognized that patterns were in some ways a more interesting concept than code reuse, in that they involved design, something much more abstract and conceptual than code.

In spite of the excitement about patterns, it is not obvious that they have had a major impact in the form of changed practice. There are probably two reasons for that.

1. Practitioners, as I noted earlier, had already been doing this kind of thing.

2. Initially, at least, most published patterns were so-called housekeeping (rudimentary, nondomain-specific) patterns. The need to find domain-specific patterns is gradually being recognized and satisfied.

This particular fact has its own interesting corollary:

Design patterns emerge from practice, not from theory.

Gamma and his colleagues (1995) acknowledge the role of practice, saying things like "None of the design patterns in this book describes new or unproven designs . . . [they] have been applied more than once in different systems" and "expert designers . . . reuse solutions that have worked for them in the past." This is a particularly interesting case of practice leading theory. Practice provided the notion of, and tales of the success of, something that came to be called patterns. Discovering this, theory built a framework around this new notion of patterns and facilitated the documentation of those patterns in a new and even more useful way.

Controversy

The notion of design patterns is widely accepted. There is an enthusiastic community of academics who study and publish ever-widening circles of patterns. Practitioners value their work in that it provides organization and structure, as well as new patterns with which they may not be familiar.

It is difficult, however, to measure the impact of this new work on practice. There are no studies of which I am aware as to how much of a typical application program is based on formalized patterns. And some say that the overuse of patterns (trying to wedge them into programs where they don't fit) can lead to "unintelligible . . . code, . . . decorators on top of facades generated by factories."

Still, since no one doubts the value of the work, it is safe to say that design patterns represent one of the most unequivocally satisfying, least forgotten, truths of the software field.

Sources

In recent years, a plethora of books on patterns has emerged. There are almost no bad books in this collection; anything you read on patterns is likely to be useful. Most patterns books, in fact, are actually a catalog of patterns collected on some common theme. The most important book on patterns, the pioneer and now-classic book, is that by Gamma et al. This book with its collection of authors has become known as the "Gang of Four." It is listed in the References section that follows.

References

➥ Gamma, Erich, Richard Helm, Ralph Johnson, and John Vlissides. 1995. *Design Patterns.* Reading, MA: Addison-Wesley.

➥ Visser, Willemien. 1987. "Strategies in Programming Programmable Controllers: A Field Study of a Professional Programmer." Proceedings of the Empirical Studies of Programmers: Second Workshop. Ablex Publishing Corp.

COMPLEXITY

Fact 21	For every 25 percent increase in problem complexity, there is a 100 percent increase in complexity of the software solution. That's not a condition to try to change (even though reducing complexity is always a desirable thing to do); that's just the way it is.

 ### Discussion

This is one of my favorite facts. It is a favorite because it is so little known, so compellingly important, and so clear in its explanation. We've already learned that software is very difficult to produce and maintain. This fact explains why that is so. It explains a lot of the other facts in this book, as well.

- Why are people so important? (Because it takes considerable intelligence and skill to overcome complexity.)

- Why is estimation so difficult? (Because our solutions are so much more complicated than our problems appear to be.)

- Why is reuse-in-the-large unsuccessful? (Because complexity magnifies diversity.)

- Why is there a requirements explosion (as we move from requirements to design, explicit requirements explode into the hugely more numerous implicit requirements necessary to produce a workable design)? (Because we are moving from the 25 percent part of the world to the 100 percent part.)

- Why are there so many different correct approaches to designing the solution to a problem? (Because the solution space is so complex.)

- Why do the best designers use iterative, heuristic approaches? (Because there are seldom any simple and obvious design solutions.)

- Why is design seldom optimized? (Because optimization is nearly impossible in the face of significant complexity.)

- Why is 100 percent test coverage rarely possible and, in any case, insufficient? (Because of the enormous number of paths in most programs and because software complexity leads to errors that coverage cannot trap.)

- Why are inspections the most effective and efficient error removal approach? (Because it takes a human to filter through all that complexity to spot errors.)

- Why is software maintenance such a time consumer? (Because it is seldom possible to determine at the outset all the ramifications of a problem solution.)

- Why is "understanding the existing product" the most dominant and difficult task of software maintenance? (Because there are so many possible correct solution approaches to solving any one problem.)

- Why does software have so many errors? (Because it is so difficult to get it right the first time.)

- Why do software researchers resort to advocacy? (Perhaps because, in the world of complex software, it is too difficult to perform the desperately needed evaluative research that ought to precede advocacy.)

Wow! It wasn't until I began constructing this list that I really realized how important this one fact is. If you remember nothing else from reading this book, remember this: For every 25 percent increase in problem complexity, there is a 100 percent increase in the complexity of the software solution And remember, also, that there are no silver bullets for overcoming this problem. Software solutions are complex because that's the nature of this particular beast.

Controversy

This particular fact is little known. If there were greater awareness, I suppose there would be controversy as to its truth, with some (especially those who believe that software solutions are easy) claiming that whatever solution complexity exists is caused by inept programmers, not inherent complexity.

Source

➡ Woodfield, Scott N. 1979. "An Experiment on Unit Increase in Problem Complexity." *IEEE Transactions on Software Engineering,* (Mar.) Finding this source caused me more work than any other in this book. I looked through my old lecture notes and books (I was sure I had quoted this somewhere else), used search engines, and e-mailed so many colleagues I think I must have begun to annoy some of them (none had heard of this quote, but all of them said they wished they had). In the final analysis, it was Dennis Taylor of IEEE who found the correct citation and Vic Basili of the University of Maryland who got a copy of the paper for me. Thanks!

Fact 22	Eighty percent of software work is intellectual. A fair amount of it is creative. Little of it is clerical.

Discussion

Through the years, a controversy has raged about whether software work is trivial and can be automated, or whether it is in fact the most complex task ever undertaken by humanity.

In the trivial/automated camp are noted authors of books like *Programming without Programmers* and *CASE—The Automation of Software* and researchers who have attempted or claimed to have achieved the automation of the generation of code from specifications. In the "most complex" camp are noted software engineers like Fred Brooks and David Parnas. In spite of the extremely wide diversity of these opinions, there have been few attempts to shed objective light on this vitally important matter. It was almost as if everyone had long ago chosen up sides and felt no need to study the validity of his or her beliefs. This fact, however, is about a study that did just that. (It is also, by the way, a wonderful illustration of another raging controversy in the field: Which is more important in computing research, rigor or relevance? I will return to that secondary controversy when I finish dealing with the first.)

How would you go about determining whether computing work was trivial/automatable or exceedingly complex? The answer to that question, for this piece of research at least, is to study programmers at work. Systems analysts were videotaped performing systems analysis (requirements definition) tasks. They were seated at a desk, analyzing the description of a problem that they were to solve later. I was the researcher who led this project, and examining those videotapes was a fascinating (and yet boring) experience. For vast quantities of time, the subject systems analysts did absolutely nothing (that was the boring part). Then, periodically, they would jot something down (this was also boring, but a light that made this whole thing fascinating was beginning to dawn).

After I had observed this pattern for some period of time, it became obvious that when the subjects were sitting and doing nothing, they were thinking; and when they were jotting something down, it was to record the result of that thinking. A bit more research consideration, and it became clear that the thinking time constituted the intellectual component of the task, and the jotting time constituted the clerical part.

Now things really began to get interesting. As the videotaped results for a number of subjects were analyzed, a pattern soon emerged. Subjects spent roughly 80 percent of their time thinking and 20 percent of their time jotting. Or, putting things another way, 80 percent of the systems analysis task, at least as these subjects were performing it, was intellectual, and the remaining 20 percent was what I came to call clerical. And these findings were relatively constant across a number of subjects.

Let's return for a moment to that rigor/relevance issue. This was not, as you can imagine, a terribly sophisticated research process. From a researcher point of view, it definitely lacked rigor. But talk about relevance! I could not imagine a more relevant research study than one that cast light on this issue. Nevertheless, my research colleagues on this study convinced me that a little more rigor was in order. We decided to add another facet to the research study. One weakness of the existing work was that it examined only systems analysis, not the whole of the software development task. Another was that it was empirical, relying on a small number of subjects who just happened to have been available when the study was run.

The second facet overcame those problems. We decided to look at the whole of software development by looking at taxonomies of its tasks. We decided to take those tasks and categorize them as to whether they were primarily intellectual or primarily clerical.

Now things get almost eerie. The categorization showed that 80 percent of those software development tasks were classified as intellectual and 20 percent were classified as clerical—the same 80/20 ratio that had emerged from the empirical study of systems analysis.

It would be wrong to make too much of the likeness of those 80/20s. The two facets of the study looked at very different things using very different research approaches. Likely, those 80/20s are more coincidental than significant. And yet, at least in the spirit of relevance if not rigor, it seems fair to say that it is quite possible that software development in general is 80 percent intellectual and 20 percent clerical. And that says something important, I would assert, about that trivial/automatable versus complex controversy. That which is clerical may be trivial and automatable, but that which is intellectual is unlikely to be.

There is a small addendum to this story. This research eventually evolved into an examination of the creative (not just intellectual) aspects of software development. As with the second facet of the first part of the research, we categorized the intellectual portion of those same tasks as to whether they were creative. After the amazing 80/20 finding of the first part of the research, we expected some similar lightning bolt result about how much of the software development job is creative.

We were to be disappointed. Our first problem was finding a useful and workable definition of creativity. But there is a creativity literature, and we were finally able to do that. The good news is that we did discover, according to our research, that roughly 16 percent of those tasks were classified as creative. But the bad news is that there were considerable differences among the classifiers; one thought only 6 percent of those tasks were creative, whereas another thought that 29 percent were. Regardless, it is certainly possible to say that a major portion of the work of software development is intellectual as opposed to clerical, and at least a significant but minor portion is even creative. And, to me at least, that clearly says that software work is quite complex, not at all trivial or automatable.

Controversy

There is little left to say about the controversy involved here, since the entire Discussion section is about a pair of controversies. I would like to say that, in my mind at least, this study settled the first controversy—software construction is definitely more complex than it is trivial. It also gives what I consider to be an excellent example of why rigor in research is not enough. If I had to choose between a rigorous study that was not relevant or a relevant one that was not rigorous, I would frequently choose relevance as my major goal. That, of course, is a practitioner's view. True researchers see things very differently.

In spite of my strong beliefs resulting from these studies, I have to confess that both controversies continue to rage. And, quite likely, neither will (or perhaps even should) be resolved.

In fact, the latest instantiation of the first controversy, the one about trivial/automatable, takes a somewhat different tack. Jacobson (2002), one of object orientation's "three amigos" (the three people who formed Rational Software, the company that created the United Modeling Language object-oriented methodology), takes the point of view that most of software's work is "routine." (He does this in an article analyzing the relationship between agile software processes and his UML methodology.) He cites the numbers 80 percent routine and 20 percent creative as emerging from "discussions with colleagues . . . and . . . my own experience." Obviously his 20 percent creative tracks with this fact, but his 80 percent routine certainly does not. Note that Jacobson fails to take into account the intermediate category, "intellectual," something important between creative and routine.

Source

The intellectual/clerical and creative/intellectual/clerical studies were published in several places, but they are both found in the following book:

➡ Glass, Robert L. 1995. *Software Creativity*. Section 2.6, "Intellectual vs. Clerical Tasks." Englewood Cliffs, NJ: Prentice-Hall.

Reference

➡ Jacobson, Ivar. 2002. "A Resounding 'Yes' to Agile Processes, but Also to More." *Cutter IT Journal,* Jan.

CHAPTER 2

About the Life Cycle

The term *software life cycle* refers to an organizing scheme for talking about the process of software construction. That hasn't always been the case. Although it began innocently enough, fairly soon expressions of the life cycle began to take on aspects of a religion. They became, for those so inclined, a rigid description of the steps to be taken—and the order in which they should be taken—to build good software. People called this rigid version of the life cycle the waterfall life cycle. The waterfall was a process that flowed only downstream, from one life cycle step to the next. Methodologies were built around it The more popular the waterfall cycle became among some segments of the software community, the more others realized that something bad was happening.

The bad thing about the waterfall was that it was a naive representation of a quite complex process. Those who really knew how software is built knew that good people, the ones who knew what they were doing, didn't really use that precise set of steps in that precise order. The steps were OK; it was the ordering that was the problem.

But let's step back a little and define what the life cycle is. It begins with *requirements* definition and development, when the "what" of the problem is defined and analyzed. Next comes *design*, when how the problem is to be solved is determined. Then comes *coding*, when the design is transformed into code that will run on a computer. Following that, because all of this is quite error-prone, *error removal* is performed. And finally, when all the tests have been passed, the software product is put into production, and *maintenance* begins.

Now let's return to the problems of that waterfall life cycle. Advocates claimed that software could be built in precisely that order. You defined the requirements, completely. Then, and only then, did you commence design. And only when design was complete did you begin coding. And testing followed the completion of coding. And, for heaven's sake, no product was ever put into production—and began to undergo maintenance—until the testing was finished.

It all sounds so reasonable. But, in fact, expert software developers had long known that they used a "build-a-little, test-a-little" approach. Requirements frequently changed as product development got under way. Designs had to be tried out via small segments of code to see if the conceptual design could really translate into a workable program. And, of course, those segments of code needed to be tested to make sure the coded experimental solution really worked. The experts knew that the waterfall was an unachievable ideal. They continued to build software as they always had, even when upper management was busy institutionalizing the waterfall. (Upper management liked the waterfall because it represented something that was much easier to manage than the chaotic but real software development process.)

After perhaps a decade of this kind of madness, during which experts ignored management directives and built software the way it had to be built, more rational heads stepped in. The so-called spiral life cycle began to be described in the literature, and—lo and behold—it described pretty much what those experts had been doing all along. Very quickly, in most parts of the software world, the waterfall was dismissed and some form of the spiral took its place.

But throughout all of this, the one thing that remained constant—and valid—was the steps themselves. We may now be saying that we spiraled and iterated our way through requirements and design and coding and error removal and maintenance, but in fact we still had to do all of those things. Only the strict ordering of doing them had been rearranged.

This chapter of the book is organized according to that scheme. As we proceed through this chapter, we will proceed through these life cycle steps. For each of the steps, we will present a collection of frequently forgotten fundamental facts.

- Facts about requirements. Remember what we said about requirements frequently changing? There are some pretty important facts about that phenomenon. And about how to handle problems with requirements.

- Facts about design. Design is probably the most intellectual and most creative part of the life cycle, and doing it reflects how complex the software development process really is. And so do the facts about design.

- Facts about coding. Coding is the bread and butter of the software development process. Because the process is pretty well understood, we present fewer facts about it than the other life cycle steps.

- Facts about error removal. All the intellectual challenge and complexity of the previous life cycle steps ends up with a product that rarely works out of the box. The challenge of error removal—for example, it is nearly impossible to build an error-free software product—is reflected in this collection of facts.

- Facts about testing. Although testing—executing the software product on sample data to see if it works successfully—is the bread and butter of error removal activities; it is nearly impossible to test software so thoroughly as to detect all of its errors.

- Facts about reviews and inspections. Because testing rarely succeeds at complete error removal, some static approaches, like reviews and inspections, must supplement it. But testing plus reviews and inspections still leaves us with error-prone software products. The facts about these two activities tell us a lot about how hard it is to achieve a good, high-quality software product.

- And, finally, facts about maintenance. Maintenance is the least understood, and in many ways the most important, phase of the life cycle. The facts here may represent some of the greatest surprises in this book about frequently forgotten facts.

Now—on through the life cycle. And don't worry about stepping into a waterfall along the way!

REQUIREMENTS

Fact 23	One of the two most common causes of runaway projects is unstable requirements. (For the other, see Fact 8.)

 Discussion

Runaway projects, as we saw in Fact 8, are those that spin out of control. There are lots of runaway projects in the software field. Not as many, I would hastily add, as those who believe in a "software crisis" would claim. But still, there are far too many of them.

Most often, projects that spin out of control were never in control in the first place. Fact 8 tells us that story. Poor or optimistic estimation—the belief and prediction that it will take far less time and money to build a software solution than it really will take—is one of the two major causes of runaway projects. But such projects are out of control from the very beginning, in the sense that they are working toward impossible targets, and their "failure" is a failure of estimation rather than of software development.

Unstable requirements (the evil twin of optimistic estimation), on the other hand, is a somewhat more complicated cause of runaway projects. This problem is caused by the fact that the customers and users for the software solution are not really sure of what problem they need to have solved. They may think they know at the outset, only to discover as the project proceeds that the problem they wanted to solve is too simplistic or unrealistic or something else they weren't expecting. Or they may really not know anything at the outset and are simply exploring solutions to a vague problem they know needs to be solved.

Either way, as you might well imagine, this is a hard situation for a software development team to be in. Given that it is extremely difficult to solve a known problem via software, it is nearly impossible to solve a problem whose requirements keep changing. It is no wonder that this kind of situation leads to a lot of software runaways. At the same time, it is not so surprising that requirements really are poorly understood. After all, software has been solving problems for only 50-something years, and it is being asked to tackle ever more diverse and complicated problems, many problems that could not even be conceived of as recently as a decade or two ago.

It is interesting to explore the solutions the software field has tried to employ to deal with unstable requirements. Early on, most people in the software field believed that the problem was weak software management, and the solution was to hold the line on the original set of requirements, insisting that when the software team had solved *that* problem, the customers and users would just have to accept that solution. It was during this era that computer scientists came up with the notion of formal specifications, a very mathematical way of representing those very firm requirements.

That approach really didn't work very well. The eventual solution didn't solve any problem the customers and users really needed solved, and, therefore, those solutions were ignored and eventually abandoned. All that time and money had been spent building a software solution that went straight to the refuse bin. And those beautiful but all-too-rigid mathematical requirements specifications went to the refuse bin with them. All too often, so did the relationship between the customers and the development organization.

Once software people began to realize that they had to accommodate the problem of changing requirements, entirely different solution approaches were tried. If the problem was exploring requirements to lead them toward stability, the solution was seen to be prototyping. We would build a sample solution, according to this idea, and let the users try it out to see if it was what they wanted. (There are lots of reasons for using a prototyping development approach, but here we are addressing only their use in requirements definition.) As user involvement got to be more and more intense, we developed a methodology called JAD, for Joint (with the users) Application Development to go with prototyping. (I never quite grasped the notion of development in this context—it always seemed to me that this should be called JARR for Joint Application Requirements Resolution.) Prototyping and JAD continue to be used to this day, especially when requirements are poorly understood.

Meanwhile, management had to figure out how to deal with requirements instability and the "moving target" problem. Initially, when requirements changed, management control seemed to fly out the window. But eventually management came to realize that, although they could not freeze requirements, they could insist that changing requirements lead to changing project terms and conditions. "You want new or revised features? Then let's talk about how much time and money that will cost over and above our original estimate." Unfortunately, that led us into the swampland of changing estimates while the project was in progress, which we dealt with in Fact 11 But revised estimates are the only approach to controlling changing requirements, and Fact 11 desperately needs to be overturned.

We are still exploring this problem of unstable and evolving requirements in the software field. We pretty much know what to do about it (per the earlier discussion), but we are less successful about doing those things we know we need to do. Plus, as software tackles ever more challenging and diverse projects, the fact of evolving requirements is ever more common. Many of the best-known runaway projects are those in which the users and the developers let the requirements changes get so out of hand that no solution to any problem was ever developed. (The classic case of this kind was the Denver Airport Automated Baggage Handling System [Glass 1998], where requirements changes were so profound that eventually all of the work was scrapped. To this day, the originally envisioned massive baggage handling system has never been built, and for all airlines in Denver except United, manual systems are used instead.)

There is an interesting new twist evolving on the requirements instability problem. The Extreme Programming lightweight methodology calls for a representative of the user community to reside with the software project team during development. That constant presence certainly will have an impact on the ability to spot and fix quickly any invalid or evolving requirements. The questions remain, however, how many user organizations (a) will be willing to give up a first-rate person to such a full-time task, and (b) have one person who can represent all the potentially varying viewpoints of the customers and users?

Controversy

Where once there was great controversy—there were those who wanted requirements to be held firm—now there is little. Nearly everyone accepts the fact that requirements must be allowed to change, and the only remaining disagreement is about how to keep control under those circumstances.

There is still some disagreement on the subject of formal specification. That mathematical approach is rarely used in practice, but it still tends to be taught and advocated in academe. This simply remains yet another area in which practice and theory are failing to communicate well. Theory tends to believe that practitioners are intransigent, and practice tends to believe that theorists are trying to waste their time. Based on the past history of theory/practice communication problems, it is unlikely that this aspect of the controversy will be resolved soon.

Sources

The primary sources for this fact are the same as for Fact 8.

> Cole, Andy. 1995. "Runaway Projects—Causes and Effects." *Software World (UK)* 26, no. 3. This study found that "project objectives not fully specified" was the leading cause of runaway projects, responsible for 51 percent of them (versus 48 percent for "bad planning and estimating").

> Van Genuchten, Michiel. 1991. "Why Is Software Late?" *IEEE Transactions on Software Engineering*, June. This study finds that the second leading cause of late projects was "frequent changes in design/implementation" (resulting from requirements changes), at 50 percent ("optimistic estimation" was the leading cause, at 51 percent). (Some projects have more than one cause, in case you were wondering how this could add to more than 100 percent.)

Reference

➥ Glass Robert L. 1998. *Software Runaways.* Englewood Cliffs, NJ: Prentice-Hall. This book tells the story of many runaway projects that suffered from requirements instability, including the Denver Airport Automated Baggage Handling System.

Fact 24	Requirements errors are the most expensive to fix when found during production but the cheapest to fix early in development.

Discussion

This fact is really just common sense. Of course, the longer an error remains in software (or in the product of any other discipline, for that matter), the more expensive it is to fix (and what could be longer than the time from requirements to production?). Boehm and Basili (2001) say that it is 100 times more expensive to fix errors in production that during the earliest development phases.

In software, this fact is particularly onerous. In its early days, software is amorphous, nothing more concrete than some kind of documented specification, relatively easily changed. But as time moves on, the software product becomes more and more detailed (in the design phase), more and more concrete (in the coding phase), and more and more rigid (as the code gets closer and closer to the final solution). What could have been corrected for almost nothing early on becomes far more difficult to correct later.

The message of this particular fact is quite clear and easy to understand—get those errors out of your software product as early in the life cycle as possible. So why is this a frequently forgotten fact? Because, although we all accept this fact as true, we do not seem to act on it. Getting requirements errors out early means heavy use of requirements-cleansing techniques, techniques that seem to be left out in our headlong rush to meet (often impossible) schedules. What kind of requirements-cleansing techniques? Requirements consistency checks. Requirements reviews (with customers and users analyzing and correcting miscommunications and flat-out mistakes). Requirements-driven early test case design. Insisting on testable requirements. Modeling, simulation, and prototyping to check early requirements validity. Perhaps, if you believe in them, formal specification techniques (because the formality tends to force rigor into the definition of the specs).

There are lots of ways to make sure that requirements have a maximum chance of being correct. Few of the items on that list are used on the average software project.

Controversy

There is really no controversy over the essence of this fact. As we mentioned before, it is nothing more than common sense.

The only controversy would be on what to do about it. Almost everyone has a nomination for a solution. Computer scientists would insist on formal specification techniques. Developers would put reviews at the top of their list. Testers and quality assurance people would require testable requirements and early test case construction. Systems analysts might well require modeling approaches. Extreme Programming advocates would place a customer representative on the development team.

The different opinions of different constituencies in the previous paragraph give us one clue as to the problem here. There is not unanimity on what solution to this problem is best. But the other clue, the one we hinted at a couple of paragraphs ago, the one that is really the most important, is our old archenemy, unreasonable schedules. No one wants to risk getting into requirements "analysis paralysis" (and that can indeed be a real problem). So we rush madly through the early life cycle phases, meeting or beating schedule, until we run aground at the end of the process with software that fails too often and testing that never seems to end. Bingo! There we are again, spending far too long and far too much to ferret out errors that have been lurking in the product since its very beginning.

Source

There are several sources for this particular fact. Here is one; the other is listed in the Reference section that follows.

➥ Davis, Alan M. 1993. *Software Requirements: Objects, Functions, and States,* pp. 25–31. Englewood Cliffs, NJ: Prentice-Hall. The fact is a rewording of Davis's viewpoint in this book.

Reference

➥ Boehm, Barry, and Victor R. Basili. 2001. "Software Defect Reduction Top 10 List." *IEEE Computer,* Jan. "Finding and fixing a software problem after delivery is often 100 times more expensive than finding and fixing it during the requirements and design stage."

Fact 25   **Missing requirements are the hardest requirements errors to correct.**

 Discussion

How can a requirement be missing? Because something went wrong during the requirements gathering process.

Requirements gathering is about defining the problem to be solved. But that raises the question, "how are requirements gathered?" The gathering of requirements is often, but not always, a process of human interaction. Those people who have the problem to be solved—the customers, the users, or their "business analysts"— are interviewed by representatives of the software development organization.

People who conduct these kinds of interviews are called systems analysts. Systems analysis may be a task for a jack-of-all-trades programmer or a task for specialists whose primary job is systems analysis. Either way, it is easy to see that systems analysis, involving lots of human interaction, is an error-prone activity. The potential for failing to gather important requirements is always present.

Systems analysis is the primary method for gathering requirements in the business applications domain. But there are other domains and other ways of gathering requirements. In some applications, where the software is part of some much larger system, the process of gathering requirements occurs at the overall system level before any requirements definition for the software portion of the system can happen. Those requirements, once gathered, are often written down in some formal document that describes the total system.

People who do this particular kind of requirements gathering are often known as systems engineers. Because of the diversity of problems that systems engineers may address, there has been little success in methodologizing (in the sense of routinizing) the process of systems engineering, and—although there are academic courses in the subject—it remains a disciplinary title with relatively undefined content.

Now, remember those documents that systems engineers create? One of the ways of defining the software requirements for such a system is to examine the systems documents as carefully as possible, picking out those requirements that drive the software part of the system. And this, too, is an extremely error-prone process. How can a software engineer, for example, know which systems requirements really have a software impact? In my experience, it is often necessary for the software requirements gathering process to be (a) iterative (it is difficult to be sure at first glance which requirements are relevant to the software), and (b) interactive (software requirements gatherers must interact with requirements gatherers from other disciplines to divide up the requirements properly).

We have seen, at this point, that systems analysis, as a human interaction process, is error-prone. We have also seen that systems engineering, as a multi-disciplinary process, is also error-prone. It should not be surprising that, in the midst of these error-prone processes, requirements flaws occur. And the greatest of these flaws is missing a requirement entirely.

Why are missing requirements so devastating to problem solution? Because each requirement contributes to the level of difficulty of solving a problem, and the interaction among all those requirements quickly escalates the complexity of the problem's solution. The omission of one requirement may balloon into failing to consider a whole host of problems in designing a solution.

Why are missing requirements hard to detect and correct? Because the most basic portion of the error removal process in software is requirements-driven. We define test cases, for example, to verify that each requirement in the problem solution has been satisfied. (We will see later that requirements-driven testing is a necessary but far from sufficient testing approach.) If a requirement is not present, it will not appear in the specification and, therefore, will not be checked during any specification-driven reviews or inspections; further, there will be no test cases built to verify its satisfaction. Thus the most basic error removal approaches will fail to detect its absence.

There is a corollary to this fact:

The most persistent software errors—those that escape the testing process and persist into the production version of the software—are errors of omitted logic. Missing requirements result in omitted logic.

Some years ago, struck by the complexity of the software error removal process, I vowed to study the notion of which errors were the most serious ones to software projects. My thinking was that, in this terribly complex process, effort spent on attacking serious errors would have more value than effort spent on less serious ones.

Of course, all software projects prioritize errors into various levels of severity. Those priorities range from so-called show stoppers—errors that cause the whole system to fail to work—to trivial errors, the kind that, for example, users can work around so readily that their solution can be deferred. (This is an important distinction. In spite of the cries for error-free software, nearly all complex software solutions run quite successfully with known errors. NASA's space missions, for example, are able to count the number of known errors in their successful mission software. And when Microsoft recently announced the number of errors in one of its systems and gleeful Microsoft-bashers jumped all over the company for this large error count, no one entered the fray to point out this distinction and its importance.)

But prioritization is in the eye of the beholder, and because of that, it is nearly impossible to say anything generically about the nature of high-priority errors and thus nearly impossible to devise approaches to attack those errors. I wanted something that could be more objectively examined.

As I thought about this, I came to realize that the most serious software errors—regardless of their nature or priority—are those that make it into the production version of the software. Surely those are more problematic than the ones that are caught before production, even if, as we have just seen, some production errors are more serious than others. So, I wondered, is there something special about those persistent software errors? And then I began thinking about how I could find out.

It turns out that the finding-out part was easy. I was working at the time for a leading aerospace company in a software research and development organization, and I had access to tons of software project error data. I isolated the production errors by the date of the error report, and, for several projects, I began collecting and categorizing error data.

As I analyzed the data, the plot thickened. I found that head and shoulders above all other kinds of persistent errors were something I called errors of omitted coding logic. This was the predominant category of persistent errors, at 30 percent. The next most important category was regression errors, new errors introduced by fixing older errors during the maintenance process, at 8.5 percent, a far cry from that 30 percent. It is interesting to note that the third category of persistent software errors did not contain software errors at all, but rather documentation errors (8 percent), where someone thought the software had failed but it had not.

What constituted an error of omitted logic? Such things as the failure to reset a data item to its original value after it had been used but was needed again and conditional statements with one or more conditions left out—the kinds of things that resulted from coders and designers not thinking sufficiently deeply about the problem they were addressing.

Why did these errors persist into the production version of the software? Because it is difficult to test for something that simply isn't there. Some testing approaches, such as coverage analysis, help us test all segments of a program to see if they function properly. But if a segment is not there, its absence cannot be detected by coverage approaches. Similarly, reviewers—who are very good at spotting errors in code that they are examining—may or may not so readily spot pieces of code that are totally missing.

Now, what does this have to do with missing requirements? Clearly, missing requirements will result in omitted logic. And for the same reason that it is difficult to spot instances of omitted logic, it is difficult to spot instances of omitted requirements.

Controversy

This fact and its corollary are about omissions. Controversy on this subject is largely omitted as well. The reason for the lack of controversy is that most people are simply not aware of these omissions. That is probably a serious mistake in the software field. There is a lot of mischief resulting from our failure to distinguish between the kinds of errors we in the field commit. (Note the earlier Microsoft story. Imagine the same kind of attack evolving against NASA for flying space missions with known errors.)

Sources

One source for the fact is

➡ Wiegers, Karl E. 2002. *Peer Reviews in Software: A Practical Guide.* Boston: Addison-Wesley.

This fact and some ways to address the problem are found on page 91.
The source for the corollary is

➡ Glass, Robert L. 1981. "Persistent Software Errors." *IEEE Transactions on Software Engineering,* May.

DESIGN

Fact 26

When moving from requirements to design, there is an explosion of "derived requirements" (the requirements for a particular design solution) caused by the complexity of the solution process. The list of these design requirements is often 50 times longer than the list of original requirements.

Discussion

Things get messy quite quickly in the software development process.

As requirements (the "what" of software, describing what problem is to be solved) evolve into design (the "how" of software, describing how the "what" problem is to be solved), something dramatic happens. As the designer struggles to find a solution approach, those somewhat finite problem requirements begin transforming themselves into the requirements for a solution. And what may have seemed straightforward from a problem point of view explodes into something quite complex from a solution point of view. These new design requirements are sometimes called derived or implicit requirements, in that they are derived from the explicit problem requirements. And that explosion from explicit to implicit has been found to be by a factor of at least 50!

Naturally, software designers would like to constrain this since an explosion of complexity this early in the software life cycle often dooms the ability to produce a simple solution to even the most simple-sounding problem. But this is one of those "that's just the way it is" facts. Despite the beliefs and best efforts of both software theorists and practitioners, it is nearly impossible to put the desired constraints on the requirements explosion problem. Simple design solutions are always sought, but only rarely found.

The adage that you should "use the simplest possible solution, but no simpler than that" is all too true!

There is a corollary to this fact, one that is only partly peripheral to this discussion:

> **This requirements explosion is part of the reason that it is difficult to implement requirements traceability—the tracing of the original requirements through the artifacts of the various succeeding phases—even though everyone agrees it is desirable to do so.**

For a couple of decades now, software people have sought a kind of Holy Grail. That Grail is the ability to trace from the requirements of a problem to the elements of its solution. This traceability would allow a software person to start with a requirement and identify each piece of design, code, test cases, documentation, and any other software artifacts that result from it.

There are many potential uses for such traceability. Perhaps the most useful would be the ability, given a revised requirement or an enhancement, to identify all of the elements of the software that need to be changed. This capability would be a tremendous boon, for example, for software maintainers, whose greatest problem (as we will see later) is understanding the existing software product enough to make changes to it.

Another use for traceability is backward tracing. Backward tracing, from a detail-level artifact to a more fundamental one, can be useful for such things as spotting dangling code, code that still exists in a program but is no longer satisfying any requirement. Dangling code is a more common problem than the software novice might expect. It is not a serious problem, in that dangling code can stay in a program and usually do very little harm, but still, dangling code may clog computer memory, may slow down program execution speed, and may clutter the software understanding process.

But traceability, for all its obvious desirability, has proven to be an elusive Grail. There are commercially available tools and methodologies for performing tracing, but they tend to fall short of the ultimate goals of a good traceability implementation.

Why is traceability such a problem? On first thought, it would seem that the linking of a requirement to its design and thence to its code and thence to its other artifacts would be a simple linked-list problem. And linked lists are fundamental to practicing software professionals; there is no mystery as to how to use linked lists.

But that first thought, unfortunately, is simplistic. The reason it is simplistic, as you have probably already realized, lies in that requirements explosion. It would be simple to link a requirement to the 5 or 6 design requirements that result from it. But when a requirement commonly links to 50 or more design requirements and each of those links to some very much larger number of coding elements and coding elements may be reused to satisfy more than one requirement, we get a burgeoning complexity problem that has resisted manual solution and even tended to thwart most automated solutions.

Controversy

This is another one of those "ignorance is bliss" facts. There is very little controversy about this fact because it is little known. What makes it a frequently forgotten fact, in spite of this ignorance, is that this particular fact has been around for decades now. I can remember teaching this subject to my software engineering graduate students at Seattle University in the early 1980s.

Note the linkage between this fact and Fact 21, the one about increases in problem complexity resulting in dramatic, even exponential, increases in solution complexity. Just as that fact is little known, so is this one. The things we said about controversy in Fact 21 could equally well apply here—that those who are determined to believe that building software is easy will simply be unable to accept this fact.

Sources

The requirements explosion problem was first identified a couple of decades ago in a study by Mike Dyer, then of IBM's System Integration Division (Glass 1992). The subject of traceability has been around even longer. (There have been ample opportunities over those years to find a workable solution to the traceability problem.) Other sources for this fact are

➡ Ebner, Gerald, and Hermann Kaindl. 2002. "Tracing All Around in Reengineering." *IEEE Software*, May. An optimistic recent revisitation of the subject of traceability.

➡ Glass, Robert L. 1982. "Requirements Tracing." In *Modern Programming Practices*, pp. 59–62. Englewood Cliffs, NJ: Prentice-Hall. Excerpts from government reports prepared in the 1970s by TRW and Computer Sciences Corp. describing their practices of tracing requirements through the development of the software product.

Reference

➡ Glass, Robert L. 1992. *Building Quality Software*. Englewood Cliffs, NJ: Prentice-Hall. An informal reference to the Dyer study is found on page 55. I have tried contacting Mike Dyer to get a more specific reference, but as of this writing, I have been unsuccessful.

Fact 27   **There is seldom one best design solution to a software problem.**

Discussion

There are two key words in this fact: *one* and *best*.

Most software problems can be solved in many different ways. That takes care of the *one*. And it is extremely difficult to know whether you have found a "best" solution, even if there were one. That should take care of the *best*.

This is kind of a discouraging, but perhaps not too surprising, fact. Given a problem definition, it is unlikely that a collection of good designers will all come up with the same optimal design solution. (One of my favorite quotes in the software field is "in a room full of top software designers, if any two of them agree, that's a majority.") Recall from previous facts the complexity of the software solution process and the explosion of requirements as we move into design. That complexity and that explosion suggest that software design is a difficult and complicated process, one that does not lend itself to simple and certainly not best solution approaches.

This is a discouraging fact because it would be awfully handy if all designers had to do was poke around until they came up with a best design solution. (Although if they never happened on that solution, of course, the problem might never be solved correctly.)

Consider this fact in the context of one of the tenets of Extreme Programming. Extreme Programming suggests that a design solution should be as simple as possible. Although this fact does not disagree with that tenet, it does suggest that many problems will not have any such simple solution (Fact 28, which speaks of design complexity, makes that point even more strongly). But it also supports this tenet of Extreme Programming in another way. If there is no best design solution, then that Extreme Programming simple solution is likely to be as successful as any other (assuming that *simple* does not translate into *simplistic*).

 Controversy

The controversy about this particular fact is largely implicit. There seems to be an assumption in many circles that there can be, and often is, a single best design solution. For example, in the reuse community, some academics have proposed basing a component-search mechanism on looking for a certain problem solution. That would work just fine if most problems had but a single solution. But, in those conference presentations during which I have heard this approach for a solution to a particular problem proposed, the examples given by the speakers generally use a solution approach that would not be the one that first occurred to me for solving that problem. Note that if one is trying to find a solution to a problem (which is what reuse is normally about) and if one's idea of the solution does not match that of the component writer, it will be hopeless to find that particular component by a solution-driven approach.

Still, most software practitioners with any significant experience at design work would agree with this fact.

Sources

It was Bill Curtis who said at a software engineering conference that "in a room full of top software designers, if any two of them agree, that's a majority."

Probably the best sources of material on design in general, and this fact in particular, are those prepared by Curtis and his colleagues at the MCC (Microelectronics and Computing Consortium), and Elliott Soloway and his colleagues at Yale University, both well over a decade ago. At the time, both groups were engaged in empirical studies of best design practices. Curtis's people, at least, were doing so with the hope of building a toolset to support and perhaps even automate the design process they identified in their research. Unfortunately, the finding of both groups was that the design process is opportunistic, which means many things (one of those meanings is a kind of opposite of *orderly* or *predictable)*, but in this context it meant that it was nearly impossible to build any such toolset. I am not aware of any concerted research effort in this area since the end of the Curtis and Soloway studies.

➥ Curtis, B., R. Guindon, H. Krasner, D. Walz, J. Elam, and N. Iscoe. 1987. "Empirical Studies of the Design Process: Papers for the Second Workshop on Empirical Studies of Programmers." MCC Technical Report Number STP-260-87.

➥ Soloway, E., J. Spohrer, and D. Littman. 1987. "E Unum Pluribus: Generating Alternative Designs." Dept. of Computer Science, Yale University.

Fact 28	Design is a complex, iterative process. The initial design solution will likely be wrong and certainly not optimal.

Discussion

Fact 27 describes the work of Bill Curtis and Elliott Soloway, and their respective teams, in analyzing the nature of software design. I mention in Fact 27 the notion of opportunistic design in which a design solution is pursued not in an orderly, predictable, and structured fashion, but in another way entirely.

That other way could be characterized in many different ways, but I choose to characterize it as "hard-part-first." Top designers pursue a design solution not by working in an ordered and top-down (or even bottom-up) fashion, but by pursuing targets of important opportunity. And those targets of opportunity are usually the difficult problems, the ones for which the designer sees no immediate solution. To see that there is a solution to the overall problem design, the designers must eliminate those areas of doubt, the subareas in which design appears to be difficult.

After all, one of the activities of the design phase is determining feasibility—is it possible to solve this problem at all? (Interestingly, as we saw in Fact 14, the result of most software feasibility studies is "yes, there is a feasible solution," even when the software engineers later discover that there really wasn't one at all.)

Let me give you an example of opportunistic, hard-part-first design. Do you recall in Fact 18 my story of developing a generalized report generator? At that time, I had never written any specific report generators. The hard problem, as I analyzed the tasks of building a report generator solution, was the notion of developing totals of columns of numbers, then totals of those totals, and even more totals of totals of totals. I called this problem "rolling totals." As I began the design process for my report generator, once I had scoped out the overall problem to see what a solution might look like, I quickly homed in on the very detailed rolling totals problem. And it wasn't until I had a solution to that particular problem that I felt comfortable in going back to the overall problem and beginning to solve it. And, of course, my rolling totals design solution played a key role in how I solved the overall problem.

Besides "opportunistic," there was another telling finding to the Curtis and Soloway work. When expert designers got right down to the nitty-gritty of design work, their approaches turned out to be heuristic, trial and error. Conceive a design solution (perhaps based on a previous design for a related problem). Mentally feed some representative data into that solution. Mentally simulate the solution operating on that data. Mentally extract the output from that data in that solution. And determine whether that output is correct. (The process is mental—"cognitive"—because often the human solution process can't wait for slower physical processes, such as scratch paper or simulations.)

Occasionally, that initial output will be correct, and that candidate solution can be considered successful in the context of that sample data. If so, try some more sample input data, and repeat the process. Eventually the data space will have been sufficiently covered, and the candidate design can be considered the real design. Much more often, the output will be incorrect. In that case, the candidate solution is wrong. Tinker with the candidate to eliminate the problem just identified. Try that sample input data again. Repeat until the output is correct. Then go back to the first three sentences in this paragraph and repeat that process.

Far from being a predictable, structurable, routinizable process, design—according to the findings of Curtis and Soloway (1987)—is a messy, trial-and-error thing. And remember, these findings are the result of studying top designers at work. One can imagine less than top designers using an even messier process. Probably the worst possible design approach, and yet one that is tempting to most design novices, is "easy-part-first." Although it is easy to get the design process started with this approach, it all too often leads to solutions-in-the-small that won't integrate into an overall solution-in-the-large. As a result, those solutions-in-the-small must often be discarded.

It is easy to see from all of this that design is complex and iterative. (This thought is explicit in Wiegers [1996].) In fact, it is probably the most deeply intellectual activity of the software development process. It is also easy to see that the initial design solution is quite likely to be wrong. And what about optimal? Well, certainly initial design solutions will rarely be optimal. But that word raises another interesting question—is there such a thing as an optimal design solution?

In a way, that question has already been asked and answered by Fact 27, wherein we discovered that there is seldom a best design solution. But there is another piece of input here that is highly relevant. For complex processes, we learned from Simon (1981) that optimal design is usually not possible, and we must strive instead for what Simon calls a "satisficing" solution. Satisficing (rather than optimizing) solutions are those that can be seen to satisfy enough of the criteria for a good design that it is worth taking the risk of choosing that approach and proceeding with problem solution, given that an optimal design is likely to be either impossible or not cost-effective to find.

Controversy

It is hard for many people, especially methodologists, to give up on the notion of orderly, predictable design and accept the notion of opportunistic design instead. Not only is that approach less intellectually satisfying, but if we document the design process instead of the design solution, we find it nearly impossible for the design documentation to be understood (because one person's set of hard-part-first problems may not be the same as someone else's). In fact, some famous computer scientists have recommended "faking" the design process (Parnas and Clements 1986), describing it as if it had been structured, even though it was not, in order to allow the resulting design documentation to be usable.

It is hard for other people to give up on the notion of design simplicity. For example, the notion of simple design is espoused in some of the new methodologies, such as Extreme Programming (XP) and Agile Development (AD) (they suggest seeking the simplest design solution that could possibly work). Certainly, for some kinds of very simple problems the design probably can be made simple. But for problems of substance, the XP/AD approaches harbor serious dangers.

And that leaves us with the notion of optimal design. There are a few people who believe in seeking and achieving optimal design, particularly those who espouse scientific approaches to the problems of business applications (for example, so-called management scientists). But all too often those optimality-seeking, scientific approaches work only for a vastly simplified version of the real problem being undertaken. In those circumstances, a solution may, in fact, be optimal but at the same time be useless.

Sources

The references to the Curtis and Soloway materials are found in Fact 27's Source section. Another place where some of that material is summarized and elaborated is in Glass (1995). The Simon (1981) material is classic, and I strongly recommend that the reader who is even slightly interested in this subject matter read that book.

References

➥ Glass, Robert L. 1995. *Software Creativity*. Englewood Cliffs, NJ: Prentice-Hall.

➥ Parnas, David L., and Paul C. Clements 1986. "A Rational Design Process: How and Why to 'Fake It.'" *IEEE Transactions on Software Engineering,* Feb.

➥ Simon, Herbert. 1981. *The Sciences of the Artificial.* Cambridge, MA: MIT Press.

➥ Wiegers, Karl E. 1996. *Creating a Software Engineering Culture.* p. 231. New York: Dorset House.

CODING

Fact 29

Programmers shift from design to coding when the problem is decomposed to a level of "primitives" that the designer has mastered. If the coder is not the same person as the designer, the designer's primitives are unlikely to match the coder's primitives, and trouble will result.

Discussion

The transition from design to coding is generally thought to be a smooth one. And, for the most part, it is—as long as the person who did the design is the same person who does the coding. But in some software organizations there are fairly strict divisions of labor. Systems analysts or systems engineers do the requirements work. Designers do the design work. And coders do the coding work. (At those organizations, testers do the testing work later—but that's a story for another time.) Sometimes, those tasks are done by in-house groups. Other times, there is outsourcing involved.

When this division of labor happens, it becomes important to talk about how best to make that hand off from design to code. Usually, a designer is expected to design down to a level where the units to be coded are so-called primitives— fundamental software units that are well known and easily coded. That sounds very simple. But, in fact, it is really simplistic. Problems arise because different people have different sets of primitives. What is a fundamental software unit to one person may not be to another.

Remember my story in Fact 18 about the first time I wrote a report generator program? To me, the most difficult task was figuring out how to do what I called rolling totals. I spent a lot of design effort on that before I was ready to begin coding. But to those who have coded a million report generators—and most business systems programmers have—that would be a trivial problem. The primitive for those skilled people would be far different—at a far higher level of abstraction—from my inexperienced level of primitive. Skilled and experienced business systems programmers would have stopped designing and moved to coding far earlier than I did.

And there's the rub. If a designer has a higher level of primitives than a coder, the resulting design will be inadequate as a starting point for the coder. Because of that, the coder will have to spend some time adding additional levels of design before being able to code. The hand off will be clumsy at best, and perhaps even troublesome, since the coder may not end up with the complete design solution that the designer expected.

The opposite problem is equally troubling. If the designer is inexperienced, as I was in my story, then he or she will develop a very detailed level of design. But a coder who has more experience than this designer will tend to reject this overly thorough level of design, discard the carefully-thought-out design work, and substitute his or her own design ideas. It is not a matter of designers needing to be smarter or more skilled than coders. It is a matter of the two having the same background or primitives.

What seemed at first glance like a simple solution—dividing the labor of designing from coding and handing off well-known primitives to bridge that gap—has suddenly become complicated. And, unless the designer and coder have approximately the same levels of primitives—an unlikely phenomenon, especially given those facts that suggest that there is no single best design solution to most problems—the transition will be far from smooth.

In my opinion, because of this fact, it is generally a mistake to engage in the separation of design work from coding work. McBreen (2000) agrees, saying "the traditional division of labor does not work in software development." Of course, for huge problems, there may be no choice.

Controversy

Like many other facts in this book, there is little controversy about this fact because it is poorly understood. I have never heard an organization that attempted the separation of design and code labor discuss this particular problem. Perhaps that's because, in most organizations that do so, designers and coders have roughly the same backgrounds. Or perhaps it is because the designers know the primitive levels of the coders so well that they can produce designs that meet the needs of the coders.

Those organizations that do separate design from coding may also do so because of the "ramping up" factor. On large projects, typically a small cadre of highly skilled people do the early requirements and design work, and only when the design is well fleshed out is a team of coders brought on board. (Note that, under these circumstances, the motivation is not so much division of labor as control of labor costs.) Thus this phenomenon will occur much more often on large projects than on small ones. And in many ways, under these circumstances, the problem of designer/coder mismatch is unavoidable—it is a mistake (and a morale destroyer) to bring a bunch of coders on board a project before there is anything for them to do.

The world of Web software has created a whole new software culture. In that culture, projects are small (people speak of 3x3 projects—three people for three months) and highly time-pressured. Under those circumstances, there is often no design at all—small projects have small design needs—and this problem seldom arises. That's why, for example, there is no mention of this problem in the Agile Development or Extreme Programming worlds—advocates for those approaches even question the need for any design at all, on some occasions!

Source

As mentioned earlier, this fact is seldom discussed in the literature. The only source I am aware of is a self-citation.

➥ Glass, Robert L. 1995. "Ending of Design." In *Software Creativity*, pp. 182–83. Englewood Cliffs, NJ: Prentice-Hall.

Reference

➥ McBreen, Pete. 2002. *Software Craftsmanship.* Boston: Addison-Wesley.

Fact 30	COBOL is a very bad language, but all the others (for business data processing) are so much worse.

Discussion

Time was when programming languages were application-domain-specific. There was Fortran, for scientific applications. There were a variety of languages, eventually Ada, for real-time applications. There was an even larger variety of languages, including something called SYMPL (for "system programming language"). There were RPG and later SQL for report generation. There was assembly language, when all else failed.

And then there was COBOL. Poor old, much maligned COBOL. COBOL was invented for business application programming. It was to be the language that was not only writeable, but readable. The saying at the time of its invention was that "grocery clerks could write it, and managers could read it" (meaning that COBOL programs could be written by unskilled people and read by anyone who might need to read them).

That obscure (and, as it turned out, unreachable) goal accounts for much that is good about COBOL, and much that is bad about it. Probably the best illustrative example is the language feature MOVE CORRESPONDING. It takes 16 characters to write, part of the reason that COBOL is thought of as the most verbose programming language ever. But it also performs a multitude of tasks—it causes data with related names to be moved from one data structure to another, doing the work of, for example, several individual MOVE statements.

But the most important thing about COBOL is that it contained (and contains) most of the language features that a business programmer might need. Fixed format data structures, for most business applications and easily specified report generation, from those data structures. File manipulation, for several different types of files and decimal arithmetic, for accounting applications. For the data and file features, it allowed vastly simplified manipulation of file data, manipulation that no other languages of its time provided (and many still don't). For the decimal arithmetic feature, it provided the penny-accurate calculations so essential to accountants and so impossible with most other numeric formats, including floating point. (For a further explanation of these language features, see the *Software Practitioner* references listed in the Source section that follows.)

Something odd happened to the programming language field after the invention of most of the domain-specific languages in the 1950s. It became unpopular to define languages that were domain-specific. Starting in the 1960s with IBM's PL/1 (it deliberately tried to satisfy the needs of all domains), language designers have tried a one-size-fits-all approach, defining languages that could be domain-independent. Never mind that PL/1 was met with derision—it was called the kitchen-sink language because it contained any language features anyone had ever thought of (and, presumably, the proverbial kitchen sink). PL/1 set the pattern for the Pascals and Modulas and Cs and Javas to come. (Ada, originally designed as a real-time language, eventually succumbed to the one-size-fits-all goal also and, arguably, died when it left those roots behind.) Few even consider the possibility of specific features for specific domains any more. (There are some conferences and publications devoted to application-specific languages, and Hunt and Thomas [2000] advocate "domain languages," but they are far from computing's mainstream, and no language of common usage seems to have emerged from that movement.)

The result of that strange history is that COBOL pretty well stands alone as the language of choice for business applications. That choice is made difficult, however, by the fact that COBOL is derided as cumbersome and obsolete and, well, name any other term of derision for a programming language, and COBOL has been called that! Each year, practitioner surveys show that COBOL usage will be considerably lowered the following year. And each year, COBOL is found to be the language with the largest increase in usage.

Controversy

There is so much distaste for COBOL that it takes a brave person to say anything positive about it. In many ways, COBOL is the laughingstock of the computing field. But the fact that its usage continues, year after year, decade after decade, suggests that the last laugh will be on those who continue to predict its demise. (It is estimated that there will be 50 billion or more lines of COBOL code next year!)

My own favorite way to describe COBOL is to paraphrase the Winston Churchill description of democracy as a political system: "COBOL is a very bad language, but all the others (for business data processing) are so much worse."

Sources

There are pockets of support for COBOL, in spite of the derision laid on it. Perhaps the largest pocket is a group that publishes newsletters, creates Web sites, and holds conferences on COBOL. The publication and Web site is called *COBOL Report,* and it is a rich and ongoing fount of COBOL knowledge. As COBOL grows over the years (the language is maintained by an organization that proposes, studies, and eventually approves updates to the language, including "modern" features such as object orientation and Web support), *COBOL Report* keeps its community aware of the latest COBOL happenings.

A few years ago, struck by the continuing usage of COBOL in spite of its naysayers, I analyzed what it offered that contemporary languages do not. That analysis resulted in a series of special issues of my own newsletter, the *Software Practitioner:*

- Sept.–Oct. 1996, such articles as "How Does COBOL Compare with the 'Visual' Programming Languages?" and "Business Applications: What Should a Programming Language Offer?"
- Nov–Dec. 1996, such articles as "How Does COBOL Compare with C++ and Java?" and "How Best to Provide the Services IS Programmers Need."
- Jan.–Feb. 1997, such articles as "COBOL: The Language of the Future?" and "Business Applications Languages: No 'Best' Answer"

Another source of (backhanded) support for COBOL is found in the following, an antisoftware engineering book that claims that "software engineering has been trying to kill COBOL for decades."

➥ McBreen, Pete. 2002. *Software Craftsmanship.* Boston: Addison-Wesley.

Reference

Hunt, Andrew, and David Thomas. 2000. *The Pragmatic Programmer.* Boston: Addison-Wesley.

ERROR REMOVAL

Fact 31   Error removal is the most time-consuming phase of the life cycle.

Discussion

This is the only phase of the software life cycle where the name comes in for serious disagreement. In an earlier draft of this book, I called it "checkout" (because that's what I called it in some of my books on software quality). I examined other books on software engineering and found that many people call it "testing," while others call it "verification and validation." Fortunately, it doesn't much matter what we call it. What matters is what is happening at this point. I chose "error removal" simply because that's the most descriptive name for this activity. This is the place in software development where the concentration is on getting the errors out.

But what is really important about this phase is that it takes longer to do error removal, for most software products, than it does to gather the requirements or do the design or code the solution—just about twice as long, as a matter of fact.

That has almost always come as a surprise to software developers. Looking forward from the beginning of the life cycle, it is easy to visualize the tasks of requirements, design, and coding. Something tangible and at least partially predictable happens in each of those phases. But during the error removal phase? What happens there is totally dependent on how the preceding phases have gone. And, often as not, they have not gone as well as the developer had expected.

Early in the history of software, grizzled old-timers (in those days, they had probably been in the field for all of a couple of years) used to bet newbies that their software would not be error-free when error removal began. And those newbies, not yet dry behind their software ears, would take the old-timers up on that bet. And lose—time after time! There is something in the software spirit, even for those old-timers, that wants desperately to believe that there have been no errors introduced into that sparkling new software product. And for those newbies, it was absolutely unimaginable that all their hard work had not resulted in perfection.

The data on the percentage of time spent in error removal has varied over the years, but the usual figures are 20-20-20-40. That is, 20 percent for requirements, 20 percent for design, 20 percent for coding (intuition suggests to most programmers that here is where the time is spent, but intuition is very wrong), and 40 percent for error removal (Glass 1992). (More recently, as advocates have suggested front-end loading the life cycle by putting more emphasis on requirements and design, the numbers are said to have changed to something more like 25-25-20-30.)

There is something else to be said about error removal. We are discussing it as if it were a one-time event, sandwiched in between coding and maintenance. But you no doubt remember that, with the spiral life cycle, software development really iterates through these various phases. That is especially important for error removal. It is largely true that testing is a separable activity, done after coding and prior to maintenance (although unit testing is often scattered throughout the coding process), but other kinds of error removal, such as reviews and inspections, tend to occur throughout the life cycle—various phase products are reviewed as they are produced.

Controversy

There is plenty of disbelief about this particular fact. It is still hard even for me to imagine, after all my years in the field, that error removal requires such a large percentage of our time. But it is important to overcome that disbelief. This fact is part and parcel of the overwhelming truth we see accumulating in this book—that the construction of software is an exceedingly difficult and error-prone task. Wishes and "breakthroughs" and "silver bullets" will not change that.

Source

The book cited in the Reference section points to lots of other sources to substantiate this fact.

Reference

➥ Glass, Robert L. 1992. *Building Quality Software.* Englewood Cliffs, NJ: Prentice-Hall.

TESTING

Fact 32

Software that a typical programmer believes to be thoroughly tested has often had only about 55 to 60 percent of its logic paths executed. Using automated support, such as coverage analyzers, can raise that roughly to 85 to 90 percent. It is nearly impossible to test software at the level of 100 percent of its logic paths.

Discussion

The literature on software testing is rich with descriptions of approaches to take in testing. (Here, we define testing as the execution of a software product to identify errors.) But it is not terribly consistent in how it describes and categorizes and even advocates those approaches.

For the purpose of this discussion, I will identify these testing approaches:

- Requirements-driven testing (testing to see if each requirement is met)
- Structure-driven testing (testing to see if all pieces of the as-built software function correctly)
- Statistics-driven testing (random testing to see how long or how well the software can execute)
- Risk-driven testing (testing to see that the primary risks are handled properly)

This fact is about structure-driven testing. But before we elaborate on this fact, it is important to say a bit about how these testing approaches should be employed.

Requirements-driven testing is necessary but not at all sufficient. All software should undergo thorough requirements-driven testing. But, in part because of the requirements explosion mentioned earlier, requirements-driven testing is never enough. As the (exploded) design requirements are converted into code, there are many parts of the software product that simply will not be executed if only the explicit requirements are addressed.

That brings us to structure-driven testing. To test those exploded bits that are not sufficiently well tied to the original requirements, it is necessary to attempt to test all of the structural elements of the as-built program. We say "attempt" because, as we will see, it is simply not possible to test all of the structure. We say "structural elements" because, although the most successful structural approach is based on logic segments, there are those who also advocate a data flow (instead of logic) approach.

Note that I am saying very little, at this point, about statistics-driven and risk-driven testing. The former is useful for giving potential users confidence that the software is ready for production use; the latter is vital for high-risk projects in which it is important to be sure that all risks are identified and handled. But given the complexity of doing thorough requirements- and structure-driven testing, these other approaches tend to be used only on projects with critical or otherwise unusual reliability needs. For more information on statistics- and risk-driven approaches see, for example, Glass (1992).

In this book I assume that structure-driven testing is about logic segments, not data flows (data flow structure adds significant complications to the testing process and is seldom used in practice). Even having said that logic segments are to be the unit of test, that still leaves the open question of "what is a logic segment?" We could test every statement or every logic path or every module/component. Module/component testing is usually a required part of structure-driven testing, but—once again—it is not enough (because within a module or component there are still lots of bits of software to be tested). As it turns out, even statement-level testing is not enough. (This counterintuitive finding requires more discussion than I am willing to devote to it here. To understand why statement-level testing is not as strong as logic path testing, see, for example, Glass [1992].)

That leaves us with logic paths. What I will talk about in the remainder of this fact is the attempt to test all program logic paths. (Often this is also called branch testing, in that it requires the testing of paths defined by logic branches. I prefer logic paths because we are not testing branches; we are testing the code between the branches.)

Now let's talk about structural test coverage. Research studies have found that, when a programmer says that code has been thoroughly tested, often only about 55 to 60 percent of its logic paths have actually been executed (Glass 1992). This testifies, as does much of the material in this fact, to the complexity of the software product, and it shows how little even the creators of a piece of software understand what they have done. Experts in logic path testing approaches say that, using tools to help identify structural test coverage (they are called test coverage analyzers), it is possible to increase this to 85 to 90 percent (Glass 1992). Counterintuitively, once again, it is often simply impossible to increase the level of logic path testing to 100 percent (because of such obscurities as inaccessible logic paths, exception cases handlers that are difficult to trigger, and so on). Those same experts advocate using inspection approaches to cover the logic paths that have not been executed. (For more on inspection approaches, see the Reviews and Inspections section beginning with Fact 37.)

What we see here is that, in spite of the plethora of testing approaches, the complexity of the typical software product defeats any attempts to do exhaustive testing. Because of that, (a) testing is an act of compromise, and it is vital to make the proper compromise choices, and (b) it is not surprising that most significant software products are released with errors remaining in them (only the naive expect error-free software).

Controversy

In spite of the rich knowledge in the field about software testing, testing in practice is surprisingly simplistic. Most software undergoes requirements-driven testing. But very little software undergoes any kind of systematic structure-driven testing. (Most programmers try to address the structural aspects of the software they have built—they understand that requirements-driven testing is not enough—but they seldom use any kind of structural analysis tools to determine how well they have done). Statistics-driven and risk-driven approaches are also seldom used in practice.

The problem here is not so much that there is controversy about this fact and its implications, but that there is almost always insufficient attention paid to the testing portion of the software life cycle. Unfortunately, it is easy to explain why that is so. The software team, as we have already seen, is working with too few resources to some sort of impossible schedule. The schedule crunch really hits home during the latter portions of the life cycle, precisely when testing is occurring. As a result, in the testing process corners that would rarely be cut in earlier life cycle phases are cut. Not only are test coverage analyzers seldom used (we will return to this thought), but there seems to be no motivation among either practitioners or their managers to spend the necessary money to procure them. Many, in fact, are unaware of their existence.

In a sense, there should be deep controversy about the inadequate structural coverage testing on most software projects. The fact that there is not speaks volumes about the status of the software field, circa the early part of the twenty-first century.

The remaining controversy about this fact pertains to the notion of producing error-free software. Although many software experts claim that it is possible and chide those organizations and companies that have not achieved it, it should be obvious from the reading of this fact that only the tiniest of software projects can achieve that glorified goal. It is important, I would assert, to give up on the impossible goal of error-free software to concentrate on more realistic and achievable goals (for example, the production of software with an absence of high-severity errors).

 ## Source

I have written extensively on software testing approaches in the citation listed in the following Reference section (as well as in other places), and—despite the passage of time since that book was written—I still believe in the more thorough discussion of this fact (and some of the ones that follow) that is found there.

Reference

➥ Glass, Robert L. 1992. *Building Quality Software.* Englewood Cliffs, NJ: Prentice-Hall.

Fact 33	**Even if 100 percent test coverage were possible, that is not a sufficient criterion for testing. Roughly 35 percent of software defects emerge from missing logic paths, and another 40 percent from the execution of a unique combination of logic paths. They will not be caught by 100 percent coverage.**

Discussion

Let's suppose for the moment, despite Fact 32, that it were possible to perform 100 percent logic path test coverage. Would doing so allow us to begin to approach that elusive goal of error-free software? In this "let's suppose," let's also suppose that in performing this complete logic path testing we do all the corollary things that go with it—building worthwhile test cases, running them in good faith, examining the test results, and determining that the tests have indeed run satisfactorily. Once again, would doing this allow us to begin to achieve error-free software?

Those were the questions I asked myself a few decades ago when I first became aware of the notion of logic path structural testing and the tools, such as test coverage analyzers, that support it. At the time—and to this day—it seemed like a very important question.

Back then, I figured out a research approach to answering that question. I was working in the aerospace industry at the time, and I had access to lots of error data from lots of real aerospace projects. I decided to examine some of that error data, one error report at a time, from the point of view of this question: Would complete logic path coverage have allowed someone to detect this particular error? At best, all answers would have been "yes," and it would have begun to look like complete structure-driven testing could lead us to error-free software products.

The answer, as you could already guess from my earlier treatments of this topic, was all too seldom "yes." There were a large number of errors that thorough structural testing would not have been sufficient to detect. As I looked at error report after error report, those particular errors began to separate themselves into two major classes. Those two classes were

1. Errors of omission, in which the logic to perform a required task was simply not in the program

2. Errors of combinatorics, in which an error would manifest itself only when a particular combination of logic paths was executed

The problem with the first is obvious. If logic is not present, no amount of increased logic path coverage will detect that particular error. The problem with the second is more subtle. It is possible, I discovered from these error reports, to execute successfully each individual logic path separately, yet find that a particular combination of those successful logic paths will be erroneous. As a trivial but blatant example, suppose a variable needed in one logic path is correctly initialized in all but one of the paths that precede it. When the combination of that one path and the succeeding path is executed, the software will fail.

That naturally raises the question of how often those kinds of errors occur. Unfortunately, the answer—at least in the error databases I was examining—was "plenty." Errors of omitted logic represented 35 percent of the database of errors I was examining. (In fact, I found in a later study [Glass 1981] that a significant number of "persistent" software errors—those that eluded all test-phase attempts to detect them and persisted through to the production state of the software product—are of this type.) Combinatorics represented a quite surprising additional 40 percent. Thus 100 percent structural test coverage, far from being a step toward error-free software, is an approach that is seductive but insufficient—insufficient at the 75 percent level (that is, complete structural coverage will still guarantee us the detection of only 25 percent of the errors in a software product).

Given that at the time I was advocating the use of structural testing approaches and the concomitant use of test coverage analyzers, this was a severe personal blow to me. But I still believe it was an important finding for the field.

Controversy

I made a mistake with this particular research finding. Instead of describing it in a paper and trying to get it published, as most researchers would do, I simply included it (as it turned out, "buried it" would be more descriptive) in a book I was writing at the time (Glass 1979). As a result, this is not one of those frequently forgotten facts mentioned in this book's title. To the contrary, it is little known.

Controversy about this fact, because of that history, is more in the nature of disbelief than opposition. I can remember presenting this particular fact at a conference in Germany. One well-known member of the software engineering community in attendance openly grumbled at the conference that she had never heard of such a finding. And she was probably correct—she hadn't heard of it.

Note the further evidence here for the inability of the software field to produce error-free software. If rigorous requirements-driven testing and structure-driven testing are not enough to allow us to produce error-free software, what would be? Some have claimed that other approaches, such as formal verification or self-testing software, would allow us to do so. But no rigorous real-world research studies of any of those alternative approaches have shown that to be true.

The fact of the matter is, producing successful, reliable software involves mixing and matching an all-too-variable number of error removal approaches, typically the more of them the better. There is no known magic solution to this problem.

Source

The source of this particular fact, as mentioned earlier, is my own research study, unfortunately buried in this out-of-print book. I have repeated those findings in subsequent works, such as the following, but they are still little known.

➡ Glass, Robert L. 1992. *Building Quality Software.* Englewood Cliffs, NJ: Prentice-Hall.

References

➡ Glass, Robert L. 1979. *Software Reliability Guidebook.* Englewood Cliffs, NJ: Prentice-Hall.

➡ Glass, Robert L. 1981. "Persistent Software Errors." *IEEE Transactions on Software Engineering,* Mar. Note that by this point I had learned that it was important to publish software engineering research findings in stand-alone papers.

Fact 34 It is nearly impossible to do a good job of error removal without tools. Debuggers are commonly used, but others, such as coverage analyzers, are not.

Discussion

The tail end of the software life cycle, to quote comedian Rodney Dangerfield, "don't get no respect."

Plenty of attention is paid to the so-called front-end phases, requirements analysis and design. There are CASE tools devoted to supporting those phases. There are university courses directed toward those phases (for example, Systems Analysis and Design courses are ubiquitous). The literature is rife with discussions of ways to do the jobs of those phases better.

Not so for the back-end phases, testing and maintenance. There are tools available to support those phases (that's what this fact is about), but they are seldom used. There are almost no university courses devoted to those phases (in many universities, the life cycle seems to end after coding). The literature seems to disdain those phases, especially maintenance (there is some material on testing, but it is comparatively sparse).

Nowhere is this discrepancy more noticeable than in the subject of tools for testing. There are plenty of tools for testing. Debuggers. Coverage analyzers. Test managers. Environment simulators. Capture/replay "automated" testers. Standardized tests (in limited circumstances). Test data generators. The problem is, those tools are seldom used. They are seldom, in fact, even procured. (The tools field is famous for its shelfware—tools purchased, put on the shelf, and never used. Test tools often fail to make it to that shelf. Tools for test automation (see Fact 35) are something of an exception. Whole shelves have been filled with them.)

What's the problem? It's not that these tools are not useful. Many of the front-end tools turned out to be overhyped, undercontributing assists of marginal value. But the back-end tools, when they are employed, contribute mightily. Debuggers are invaluable for tracking down errors. Coverage analyzers are essential for structure-driven testing. Test managers dramatically reduces the clerical labor involved in repeated testing. Embedded software testing is next to impossible without environment simulators. Capture/replay, although it fails to live up to the "automated testing" claims made for it, significantly reduces the clerical aspects of test repetitions. Standardized tests, when they can be employed (such as for checking the language conformance of a compiler), are must-haves. Test data generators are vital, particularly in cases such as statistical testing, where tests must be generated and regenerated.

It's not lack of usefulness that's the problem. It's lack of attention. There are three major factors in the lack of use of test tools in software:

1. The field in general and both management and academe in particular have made the front end far more visible. There's nothing wrong with front-end visibility, of course. We have already seen that errors that arise in the front end are by far the most costly. And requirements/ design mistakes are hard to overcome. But it is not necessary, while focusing on the front end, to ignore the back end. And that is what has happened.

2. The back-end work is technically "grubby." Even if one cannot actually do analysis or design, one can imagine what doing it is all about. That is not true for testing and maintenance. There are deep technology mysteries (those are the things I call "grubby") to doing a good job of testing and maintenance, mysteries that the average superficial manager is simply uninterested in unraveling.

3. Schedule crunches are, at their worst, at the back end of the life cycle. There is often too little time to do a thorough job of testing, in particular. Slap-dash testing, in an effort to play schedule catch-up, is often the norm. Having test tools and using them take up-front attention and in-phase effort—attention and effort that are all too often unavailable.

The most rudimentary form of test tool is the debugger; and, according to research studies and practical experience, most software developers do, in fact, make use of them. But most of the other tools are totally ignored, to the point that many software developers and even more of their managers are unaware of their existence. As are many testers.

Interestingly, for the tools-ignorant there are so-called tools catalogs available from a variety of vendors, catalogs that list tools available, their sources, their prices, and the extent of their usefulness (ACR 2001). But even these tools catalogs are seldom purchased (few organizations I have visited have ever heard of them. And, as a friend of the developers of one of these catalogs, I know how much of a marketing struggle they have had.)

Perhaps the most to-the-point recent study of test tool usage (Zhao and Elhaum 2000) examined the reliability aspects of open-source software. In a survey of open-source software developers, the authors of the research found that testing was pretty Spartan. Only 39.6 percent used any test tools at all, and most of those tools were debuggers. There was almost no use of coverage analysis. Few even developed any kind of test plan.

This is not intended to pick on open-source developers. A study of traditional developers would likely show the same kind of results (test plans might be a bit more commonly used). However, the reason for the lack of tools usage by open-source developers was particularly interesting. These developers apparently expected that the "with enough eyeballs, all bugs are shallow" philosophy would flush out whatever errors were in their product. (Open sourcers expect that users of their software will read and analyze it, thus finding the errors themselves.) This philosophy, of course, may be extremely successful for software that users want to read and do read. But, if not enough eyeballs are devoted to a software product, there is every reason to expect that such open-source software may be less reliable than it should be. And the developers, of course, have no way of knowing whether enough eyeballs have been made available to them.

Controversy

As we previously mentioned, there is little attention paid to the back-end software life cycle phases. Because of that, there is little controversy about this particular fact. It's not that anyone in particular either agrees or disagrees strongly with this fact. It's not even that there is ignorance about this particular fact. What is true is simply that the same forces that make the software back end, and testing tools in particular, of too little interest also result in too little attention being paid to this matter. I suspect that if software engineers were polled on this subject, a strong majority would agree with this fact—and then shrug their collective shoulders and go about business as usual.

Source

The study of open-source software reliability, which showed a lack of tools usage, is found in the References section.

References

→ ACR. 2001. The ACR Library of Programmer's and Developer's Tools. Applied Computer Research Inc., P.O. Box 82266, Phoenix AZ 85071-2266. This was an annually updated software tools catalog. It is recently discontinued.

→ Zhao, Luyin, and Sebastian Elbaum. 2000. "A Survey on Quality Related Activities in Open Source." *Software Engineering Notes,* May.

Fact 35	Test automation rarely is. That is, certain testing processes can and should be automated. But there is a lot of the testing activity that cannot be automated.

 Discussion

Software people have dreamed of automating software processes throughout the history of the field. One by one, those dreams have been dashed.

At one point, it was the automatic generation of code from specifications. Many researchers thought it would be possible, and it wasn't until one research paper called the idea a "cocktail party myth" (Rich and Waters 1988) that most researchers began to give up on the notion. Next, CASE tools were supposed to automate much of the front end of the life cycle. But in spite of claims of "programming without programmers," and the "automation of programming," the whole idea eventually died. CASE tools were useful, but most of them became shelfware simply because they couldn't live up to the exaggerated claims that were made for them.

It was probably inevitable that the automation hypesters, once they were defeated on the front-end life cycle playing fields, would move on to the life cycle's back end. The next thing that burst on the software scene was tools to "automate" the testing process. Like most of the hype that preceded it, there was some truth to the testing automation claims. There were testing tools, and pretty good ones at that. They did contribute to the programmer's and the tester's abilities to find and remove software errors. They even automated some portions of the testing task.

But underline the words *some portions*. Various tools automated various subsets of the tester's effort, but the totality of those automations came nowhere close to automating all of testing.

- For example, capture/playback tools were pretty handy devices for recording testing inputs so that they could be rerun later if tests needed replicating (and they often do).

- For example, test managers were really handy tools for repeatedly running a set of test cases and comparing their results to a test oracle (*test oracle* is the computer science term for a set of known correct answers).

- For example, creating and handling regression test collections was an excellent way of thwarting the damaging of old and correct code when new changes were being inserted into the code.

But there were lots of vital testing tasks not automated:

- Selection of what should be tested, and how.
- Creation of test cases that maximize the number of equivalence classes that each test represents.
- Gathering expected, correct test case results to create a test oracle.
- Planning the infrastructure for the testing process.
- Determining the judgment process by which testing will be conducted and, later, deemed complete.
- Coordinating test construction, conduct, and result checking with the customers and users of the software product.
- Deciding on the compromises that maximize the choices and rewards of test technique and test conduct.

There is more. Testing, like programming before it, is far too complex a task to be fully automated. That should not prevent us from using the tools that do automate the automatable tasks. But it does mean that we should ignore any claims for complete automation of the testing process.

Controversy

At this point, the only people who claim that testing can be fully automated are vendors of testing tools. As with all vendors, their input should be taken with one or more grains of salt, and when claims of total automation are made, they should be given a deaf ear.

Notice that the underlying theme of many of the facts in this book is that the construction of software is a complex, deeply intellectual task, one that shows little possibility of being made simple. Automation is the ultimate trivialization of this nontrivial activity, and those who claim that it has been achieved are doing serious harm to the software field in its quest for better realistic tools and techniques.

 ## Sources

Lots of people have tried to stand up to the hype in our field but the hypesters persist. Perhaps the most important expression of the antihype position is from Brooks who expresses disdain for the search for the "silver bullet" that will slay the "werewolf" of software complexity.

➥ Brooks, Frederick P., Jr. 1995. "No Silver Bullet—Essence and Accident in Software Engineering." In *The Mythical Man-Month,* Anniversary ed. Reading MA: Addison-Wesley. This was published earlier as a stand-alone paper, and the book appeared several decades ago in its first edition. But in this reissue of that classic book, Brooks sets much more context for his beliefs and brings his outlook up-to-date.

One article that presents a realistic view of test automation is

➥ Sweeney, Mary Romero. 2001. "Test Automation Snake Oil." In *Visual Basic for Testers,* by James Bach. Berkeley, CA: Apress.

This book presents a collection of lessons learned on testing. Chapter 5 dispels many of the myths about automated testing.

➥ Kaner, Cem, James Bach, and Bret Pettichord. 2002. *Lessons Learned in Software Testing.* New York: John Wiley & Sons.

Reference

➥ Rich, Charles, and Richard Waters. 1988. "Automatic Programming: Myths and Prospects." *IEEE Computer* (Aug.): 40–51:

Fact 36	**Programmer-created built-in debug code, preferably optionally included in the object code based on compiler parameters, is an important supplement to testing tools.**

Discussion

In this era of automated everything, it is all too easy to leave the work of software testing to tools and techniques. But doing so would be a mistake.

There are some simple home-remedy approaches to testing that are, in many ways, the first line of testing defense. Pour over your design and code in self-reviewing desk-check mode. Enlist the assistance of your colleagues in reviewing your code. And be prepared to insert extra debugging code into the program whenever some mysterious bug taxes your desk-checking capability. The debugging process is the detective story of programming. You play Sherlock Holmes in pursuit of the elusive software bug. And, like Sherlock Holmes, you need to enlist your brain and any brain-supporting things you can think of.

Adding code to a program specifically to isolate and investigate an error may seem counterproductive, but it is all too often essential to the process. If you only knew the value of this particular variable at this particular time, it would help immeasurably in figuring out what is happening. Insert some code to display the variable's value at that time.

If it's a problem that looks persistent or if it's one of a class of problems for which the same kind of investigative tools might prove useful, consider leaving the debug code in the program semipermanently. It can be branched around when everything is going well. It can also be inserted or excerpted at compile time by appropriate use of text editor or compiler-conditional inclusion capability. Thus debug code, once created, can be kept around in case it is needed later. (Remember to test the program with the debug code turned both on and off.)

Controversy

Most programmers use these home-remedy techniques almost intuitively. But since this fact is seldom taught explicitly in beginning programming courses, it is important to at least mention it here. This is a case in which software practice understands the value of some approaches that computing theory has not encompassed.

Source

See the topics of desk checking and source language debug in the following:

➡ Glass, Robert L. 1992. *Building Quality Software.* Englewood Cliffs, NJ: Prentice Hall.

REVIEWS AND INSPECTIONS

Fact 37	Rigorous inspections can remove up to 90 percent of errors from a software product before the first test case is run.

Discussion

We have spent a lot of the preceding facts dismissing the idea that there are any breakthroughs in tools and techniques for building software. There are, we have repeatedly seen, no silver bullets.

News flash: The irony is, tucked away in the error removal activity of software, there is one technique that is as close to being a breakthrough as anything we have. Rigorous inspections—the technique of pouring over a piece of software to identify any errors it contains—constitute a near-breakthrough. Research study after research study has shown that inspections can detect up to 90 percent of the errors in a software product before any test cases have been run. And that signifies an extremely effective process.

Furthermore, the same studies show that the cost of inspections is less than the cost of the testing that would be necessary to find the same errors. What we have here is an effective process that is also cost-effective. And that's a pretty nice combination.

So why aren't inspections (they are often also called reviews, although purists will distinguish between the two) lauded in the same way that lesser "break-throughs" such as CASE tools and various methodologies have been? Here are four reasons:

1. There are few major vendors making money from inspections.

2. There is nothing new (and thus marketable) about inspections.

3. Inspections are seen as part of that largely invisible back end of the software life cycle.

4. In spite of being effective, inspections require a lot of grueling, mind-intensive hard work.

Let's take each of those reasons and expand on them a bit.

The first two reasons go together. They are about motivation. Who would be motivated to make claims of greatness for inspections? There are vendors selling courses in how to perform inspections, of course, but what they are marketing is not radically different from what they might have marketed two or three decades ago. Without an economic motivation—there are few enterprises left that want to learn more about performing inspections—the hypesters who might be right for once are simply remaining silent.

We have already discussed the third reason, the lack of attention being paid to the life cycle's back end. Inspections are simply caught up in that tendency. Never mind that inspections can be made of the products of any of the life cycle phases. They are still seen as something that happens in the back end.

The fourth reason bears some elaboration. It may seem a simple thing to conduct an inspection. It is not. Regardless of the fact that those who market inspections place a heavy emphasis on formal steps and rules and roles, it is the rigor (focused attention) with which the inspection team members approach the inspection process that determines how successful the inspection will be, not the use of formality. And that rigor has a high cost. I have participated in inspections, and about an hour of that kind of intense concentration is about all I (and others who have done so) can handle at a time. And yet, at somewhere around 100 lines of code (LOC) inspected per hour, it takes an investment of many hours to inspect even a small piece of software, say a couple of thousand LOC.

The result is that, even though the cost of an inspection is less than its alternatives, few enterprises inspect every line of every piece of software they build. Thus, once again, we see the error removal process consisting of some vitally important compromises—which portions of which code segments shall we inspect? The answer tends to be "critical portions of critical code." And the meaning of that answer is, of course, application-dependent.

There is one peculiarity about this fact that you may or may not have noted. It is impressive, of course, that any kind of technique could help find 90 percent of the errors in a software product. But that begs an interesting question: Since we rarely know how many errors are in a software product until it has been used for a considerable period of time, how can we possibly know—especially during the testing phase of software—that we have found 90 percent of them? The answer, of course, is that we cannot. Although I have never seen this discussed in one of the research studies that identified this particular fact, I think that the claim really should be "reviews commonly remove up to 90 percent *of known errors* from a software product before the first test case is run."

Controversy

Those who are aware of this fact tend not to doubt the claims made for inspections. Those who are not would have to have been ignorant of the subject for several decades, and as a result they are unlikely to form a new opinion on the subject now. Thus the only real controversy about inspections is *how* to conduct them. Most of the advocates of inspections tend to emphasize the formal, rules/roles approach. There is also an expectation by most inspection advocates that they are best conducted in a meeting setting.

But there have been enough research studies about inspections to cast doubts on those two views. Alternative inspection approaches (Rifkin and Deimel 1995) focus not on formality but on technology—learning how to read software or what kinds of things to look for. Inspections conducted by individuals have been as effective, in some circumstances, as inspections in a meeting setting. There have even been studies of the optimal number of participants if an inspection is conducted in a meeting, and that number tends to be between two and four.

There is, however, some genuine opposition to inspections, often on the grounds that they can be contentious and lead to bad team morale. Clearly, the sociological aspects of inspection must be carefully addressed.

Sources

The most pessimistic number I have seen for the percentage of errors detected by inspections is 60 percent (Boehm and Basili 2001). The Bush presentation (1989) and several other studies have claimed up to 90 percent.

There has been a lot of research ground covered in this discussion. Rather than providing a citation for each finding, I provide a source for a more elaborate discussion of this topic, in which can be found a more detailed list of such sources.

➤ Glass, Robert L. 1999. "Inspections—Some Surprising Findings." Practical Programmer. *Communications of the ACM,* Apr.

The Rifkin article listed in the References section is a particularly good example of a nonformal, high-technology alternative to the more traditional inspection approaches.

There have been many excellent books on inspections, even if most of them do tend to emphasize the formal approach. A particularly good and recent one, which does a nice job of presenting the variations on the formality theme, is

➤ Wiegers, Karl E. 2002. *Peer Reviews in Software—A Practical Guide.* Boston: Addison-Wesley.

References

➤ Boehm, Barry, and Victor R. Basili. 2001. "Software Defect Reduction Top 10 List." *IEEE Computer,* Jan.

➤ Bush, Marilyn. 1989. Report at the 14th Annual Software Engineering Workshop. NASA-Goddard, Nov.

➤ Rifkin, Stan, and Lionel Deimel. 1995. "Applying Program Comprehension Techniques to Improve Software Inspections." *Software Practitioner,* May.

Fact 38

In spite of the benefits of rigorous inspections, they cannot and should not replace testing.

Discussion

Inspections, as we have just seen, are probably the closest thing we have in software to a breakthrough technology. Well now, let's *really* dispose of the notion of breakthroughs ever really being breakthroughs.

Inspections are a potent technique. But they are by no means enough for doing a complete job of error removal. I have said it before in this book, and I will say it again (Fact 50): Error removal is a complex task, and it requires all the armament the tester can muster.

That search for the silver bullet has been just as prevalent in the error removal phase of software development as it has in all the other phases. At various times, advocates have made silver bullet claims for several error removal approaches. Computer scientists have long said that formal verification, if done sufficiently rigorously, will be enough. Fault-tolerance advocates have taken the position that self-checking software, which detects and recovers from errors, will be enough. Testing people have sometimes said that 100 percent test coverage will be enough. Name your favorite error removal poison, and someone has probably made grandiose claims for it.

But no. Software construction is a complex, error-prone activity. Errors are a devious and diverse lot. Software developers have the same human frailties as the rest of us. There is no silver bullet for error removal. Inspections, for all their glorious power, are not enough by themselves.

Controversy

There are occasional claims that 100 percent inspection effectiveness is achievable (Radice 2002). But most people know that no matter how valuable inspections really are, they cannot be the only error removal approach.

There is resistance, more than controversy, connected with this fact. Software people desperately want to believe that error-free software is possible and that the right error removal approach will make that happen. Just as we have never quit looking for the silver bullet in all the other software development areas, we will probably never quit looking for it here. And, as a result, there will be people who claim that they have found something that will make all of that miraculously possible.

Don't you believe them!

Sources

Over the years there have been several studies comparing the effectiveness of testing and reviews and inspections (Basili and Selby 1987; Collofello and Woodfield 1989; Glass 1991; Myers 1978). All of them come to the conclusion that reviews (of various kinds) are more effective, and more cost-effective, than testing. But none of them recommends the elimination of testing.

In addition, there are plenty of sources for some of our other facts that bear on this one. Recall that inspections are claimed to have found up to 90 percent of software errors (Fact 37). Recall that test coverage analysis can likely cover up to 90 percent of a software product, but that even 100 percent coverage is far from enough (Facts 32 and 33). Recall that 100 percent requirements-driven testing, because of the requirements explosion we discussed earlier, is a far cry from sufficient testing approach (Fact 32 discussed that and other testing approaches). Recall that test automation falls very short (Fact 35). Formal verification (alias proof of correctness) has been found to be as error-prone as software construction itself, and for that and other reasons it is unlikely to be that silver bullet (Glass 2002).

There is plenty of evidence to support the notion that software error removal will always have to be a multifaceted topic.

References

➡ Basili, Victor, and Richard Selby. 1987. "Comparing the Effectiveness of Software Testing Strategies." *IEEE Transactions on Software Engineering,* Dec.

➡ Collofello, Jim, and Scott Woodfield. 1989. "Evaluating the Effectiveness of Reliability Assurance Techniques." *Journal of Systems and Software,* Mar.

➡ Glass, Robert L. 2002. "The Proof of Correctness Wars." Practical Programmer. *Communications of the ACM,* July.

➡ Glass, Robert L. 1991. *Software Conflict.* Englewood Cliffs, NJ: Yourdon Press.

➡ Myers, Glenford. 1978. "A Controlled Experiment in Program Testing and Code Walkthroughs/Inspections." *Communications of the ACM,* Sept.

➡ Radice, Ronald A. 2002. *High Quality, Low Cost Software Inspections.* p. 402. Andover, MA: Paradoxicon.

<table>
<tr><td>

Fact 39

</td><td>

Postdelivery reviews (some call them "retrospectives") are generally acknowledged to be important, both from the point of view of determining customer satisfaction and from the point of view of process improvement. But most organizations do not do postdelivery reviews.

</td></tr>
</table>

 Discussion

It should not come as a surprise, based on all the previous facts in this book, that the newly released production version of a software product has problems. Nor should it come as a surprise that, during that life cycle process, several things went less well than all of the software team members would have liked.

What is a surprise is that we as a field tend to do absolutely nothing about that. Oh, we continue to pursue errors—with such approaches as alpha testing and beta testing and regression testing and more—but what we don't do is sit back, cogitate about what has happened, and make and file some notes about how to do it better in the future.

The result is that all the lessons learned on the typical software project tend to be discarded, or they flutter off on the wind when the project ends. Why? Because in the mad schedule rush that the software field is caught up in, the programmers on yesterday's project have already scattered to tomorrow's project. And there, they are too caught up in their new schedule commitments to be drawn back to think about what happened X months ago.

X months ago? Common sense says that immediately after a project ends, it may be too soon to gather up those lessons learned (because a lot of the lessons learned from product usage have not yet been gathered). Most advocates of post-project reviews (or "retrospectives," as Kerth [2001] calls them) suggest that 3 to 12 months after delivery is the best time to review what happened. But 3 to 12 months in the software field is one or more eternities. Because of this, Kerth suggests holding the review 1 to 3 weeks after a project's end; at that time, the technical aspects of the project, if not the usage aspects, can be thoroughly dealt with.

What could a postdelivery review consist of? Advocates suggest two things (actually, two different reviews): a user-focused review, which discusses what has happened with the product from a user point of view, and a developer-focused review, to allow the developers a chance to go back over what went wrong, what could have gone better, and how.

But no matter. A lot of thought has gone into what those reviews should consist of, but in today's era they are simply not going to happen. (Ironically, we seem to find the time later on to recover from repeated instances of failures that could have been prevented by coming to grips with past lessons learned.) What a shame. As a result of this one fact, the software field tends to be stuck in place, making the same mistakes on project after project. Brossler (1999) says "development teams do not benefit from existing experience, and they repeat mistakes over and over again." We talk about capturing best of practice approaches, for example, but a cursory examination of most best of practice documents will show that they have regurgitated the things that have been in most software engineering textbooks for several decades. What is missing is some fresh, oh-wow-look-what-we-did and here-is-how-we-fixed-that stuff.

Let me digress for a moment. There is more to this software-stuck-in-place thought than what I just finished saying. An Australian colleague, Steve Jenkin, suggested to me his view of the rate of progress of the software profession. Its average experience level, he said, has tended to remain constant over time. Sounds counterintuitive, doesn't it? But what he meant was that, with the explosion of newcomers arriving in this fast-growing profession, the increasing experience level of the growing-olders is more than overcome by the low experience level of the hordes of newbies. As I thought a bit about what Steve said, I came to this thought that I would like to introduce as a corollary:

The wisdom of the software field is not increasing.

If our experience level is not growing, then neither is our wisdom level. In fact, in our mad rush toward the new, we tend to discard much of the old. (For example, software's newest and most popular methodologies, like Extreme and Agile, tend to make a point of rejecting the accumulated wisdom of the older methodologies.)

What could increase that wisdom? How about capturing those "lessons learned" (IEEE 1993)? How about some postdelivery reviews? How about those Experience Factories that Vic Basili and his colleagues at the University of Maryland propose (Basili 1992; IEEE 2002)? How about some best of practice documents based on practice, not on textbooks? How about some more personal retrospectives, like those in Brooks (1995) and Glass (1998). How about placing a priority in our field on increasing our collective wisdom? In an era of knowledge management, this is one collection of knowledge that desperately needs to be captured, managed, and applied (Brossler 1999).

Controversy

Everyone who has thought about the underlying fact here knows there is a problem, but no one seems to know a practical way to do anything about it.

There is plenty of potential controversy about the corollary. In reviewing this book before publication, Karl Wiegers said, "I disagree….New people are being added to the profession without nearly as many old people departing. If you assume that the incoming people bring at least some wisdom with them, then I think the cumulative wisdom is increasing." He then went on to tell the fascinating story of how he, an experienced software engineer, and a new young hire of his blended the wisdom that each of them brought to the table.

In any case, I think most would agree that our field is so busy with its foot pressed to the gas pedal that it rarely has time to think about how it could be going better, not just faster. We speak of working smarter, not harder. But who has time to get in a position of working smarter?

And the mechanism for capturing those lessons learned is largely missing. Computer science, which could be drawing on practical lessons learned through empirical research to form new theories, seems not to be interested. It's as if the theory world is so caught up in its own things that it is not interested in examining those theoretical things in the context of practice.

 ## Sources

The sources for this fact follow.

➥ Basili, Victor. 1992. "The Software Engineering Laboratory: An Operational Software Experience Factory." Proceedings of the International Conference on Software Engineering. Los Alamitos, CA: IEEE Computer Society Press. Basili has written a great deal more on this topic in recent years and conducts seminars on the subject. Contact him at the Computer Science Dept., University of Maryland.

➥ Brooks, Frederick P., Jr. 1995. *The Mythical Man-Month*. Anniversary ed. Reading, MA: Addison-Wesley, 1995; This is the ultimate project retrospective. In this book, Brooks discusses his experiences and captures his lessons learned from one of the all-time largest software projects, the development of IBM's Operating System 360 (OS/360).

➥ Brossler, P. 1999. "Knowledge Management at a Software Engineering Company—An Experience Report." Proceedings of the Workshop on Learning Software Organisations (LSO'99).

➡ Glass, Robert L. 1998. *In the Beginning: Personal Recollections of Software Pioneers.* Los Alamitos, CA: IEEE Computer Society Press.

➡ IEEE. 2002. "Knowledge Management in Software Engineering. Special issue." *IEEE Software,* May. Contains several articles on postmortem reviews and the experience factory.

➡ IEEE. 1993. "Lessons Learned." Special issue. *IEEE Software,* Sept.

➡ Kerth, Norman L. 2001. *Project Retrospectives: A Handbook for Team Reviews.* New York: Dorset House.

Fact 40	Peer reviews are both technical and sociological. Paying attention to one without the other is a recipe for disaster.

 ### Discussion

There is one word connected to the subject of reviews that needs to be stressed for its importance. That word is *rigor.* It is vitally important that the participants in a review process be totally dedicated to and focused on what they are doing. Because of the nature of a review and because of the complexity of the software product, reviewers must concentrate harder during reviews than during almost any other part of the software development process. That concentration is the only way that the absolutely necessary rigor can be achieved.

After all, what is happening during a review is that the participants are trying to understand and follow, at an intimate level, all of the decisions and nuances of the budding software product. That's particularly difficult because a reviewer must deal with the review materials on the terms of the producer of the material, not on his or her own terms. Recall that there is seldom any one correct or optimal design solution to a problem. It is easy, during a review, to review the work product from the point of view of what your own solution approach would be, rather than the solution approach chosen by the developer. And "walking a mile in someone else's moccasins" is very difficult for most of us to do.

All of that, of course, is about technology. The issues that cause rigor to be essential and yet difficult are embedded in the technology of creating a software solution. But all of those technological difficulties create another problem.

The concentration needed to do a good technical review job tends to diminish the amount of attention we pay to the social aspects of the review. During most of our social activities, a certain percentage of our being is devoted to the topic in question, and the remainder is devoted to making the social relationship work. At a software review, that becomes difficult. The focus needed to achieve rigor eats away at the energy we have left to work the social issues. And the social issues during a review can be profound. In spite of the cries for "egoless programming," most of us have an emotional and intellectual investment in our work product, one that makes us particularly vulnerable when others are reviewing it. And when the result of a reviewer's rigorous concentration is being considered by the remainder of the review group, that reviewer also has ego on the line. With all those egos at stake and with the social defense mechanisms diminished, it doesn't take much to cause a sociological eruption.

There are various formal approaches for conducting reviews. Most of those formal approaches provide for handling the sociological problems. Don't permit managers to attend reviews (they'll tend to review the producer, not the product.) Don't permit unprepared attendees to participate (they'll upset the ones who are prepared, and cause topical digressions). Separate the review leader role from the producer role (to try to diminish the ego involvement of the producer). Hard-won sociological lessons are embedded in the rules for most formal reviews. And informal review approaches had better look out for those same problems.

I well remember my first experience with a code review. A bunch of us wanted to review a product (some code I had written) under the most favorable of circumstances (in addition to reviewing my code, we were exploring the then-new idea of code reviews). To create the most sociologically favorable environment, we met in the recreation room of one of the reviewers and declared an open refrigerator policy during the review. All of that helped, but not enough. By the end of the first (and, as it turned out, last) hour of the review, we were really getting on each other's nerves for all the reasons I mention in the preceding paragraphs. In fact, when we ended the review an hour (and just 60 lines of code) later, we had the best of intentions for getting back together to finish the job. But we never did.

Controversy

There is controversy about reviews, but it is usually more about whether to have them than about their sociological aspects. In fact, my own suspicion is that the reason there is controversy about having reviews at all is because most of us understand how difficult the sociological aspects really are.

Source

Over the years, there have been a lot of worthwhile books on the subject of reviews. But my favorite, because it is new (and, I suppose, because I participated in the book's own review process), is

➥ Wiegers, Karl E. 2002. *Peer Reviews in Software: A Practical Guide.* Boston: Addison-Wesley.

MAINTENANCE

Fact 41	Maintenance typically consumes 40 to 80 percent (average, 60 percent) of software costs. Therefore, it is probably the most important life cycle phase of software.

 Discussion

The subject of software maintenance is full of ongoing surprises to people who don't know the software field very well. First, there's the issue of what the word *maintenance* means in the software field. In most other fields, it's about repairing things that break or wear out. But the nature of software is such that it never breaks or wears out. Software is an intangible thing, having no particular physical form, and so there is not anything to break or wear out.

But software can have errors in it. And software can be modified to do new things. (That's where the *soft* in *software* comes from, in fact. It's an extremely malleable product, in part because it is so intangible.) The thing is, software's errors aren't due to material fatigue, but rather to errors made when the software was being built or errors made as the software is being changed. So software maintenance is about fixing those errors as they are discovered and making those changes as they become necessary. It all makes sense to software people, even if it doesn't to folks from other disciplines.

The second surprise is how much cost and time software maintenance consumes. The cost and time under construction of your average software product is 20 to 60 percent; the remaining 40 to 80 percent it is undergoing maintenance. (For purposes that will become apparent later in this book, we are going to say that software maintenance consumes roughly 60 percent of the software life cycle.) From a cost and time point of view, maintenance is the dominant phase of software production. All of that error correction and modification consumes a whole lot of dollars and hours. And because of that, maintenance is probably the most important life cycle phase of software.

That's pretty counterintuitive, even to software folks. Just as software people believe that their product won't have any errors in it, software people also tend to believe that, once their product is put into production, it will run undisturbed for years—or even decades. In fact, the Y2K problem was an interesting example of the role of maintenance in software. (Y2K was the need to fix software that handled years as two-digit numbers when the calendar switched from 1999 [99] to 2000 [00]. Some programs took that to mean that time had moved backwards.) There were two surprises to Y2K. The first was how pervasive the problem was. The second was how long-lasting the programs that needed to be fixed had been (many of them dated back to the 1960s or 1970s).

There's an old software saying that I'd like to make into the following corollary:

Old hardware becomes obsolete; old software goes into production every night.

Controversy

This is one of these facts that exemplifies the need for *frequently forgotten*. Software people tend to behave as if the original development of the software product is all that matters. So do academics teaching software classes. Whereas a great deal of emphasis is put on the so-called front-end life cycle phases in the practitioner and academic literature of the field, almost nothing is said about the vital maintenance activities. In fact, many companies do not collect enough data to know how much maintenance they are doing. And the computer science or software engineering curriculum that contains material on software maintenance is rare indeed.

The result of all this forgetting is that otherwise knowledgeable people often say absolutely crazy things about maintenance. We will see what some of those absolutely crazy things are in the discussion surrounding the next fact. That fact will also deal with the obvious question, "how much of that software maintenance is about error correction, and how much is about modification?" If you're betting on error correction, you're in for another one of those ongoing surprises.

 ## Sources

This fact has been known for a long time. The first people to put it into print in the software literature did so 30-something years ago. And have been resaying it ever since. So there is really no excuse for forgetting this fact. But people do it all the time.

→ Boehm, Barry W. 1975. "The High Cost of Software." In *Practical Strategies for Developing Large Software Systems*, edited by Ellis Horowitz. Reading, MA: Addison-Wesley.

➡ Lientz, Bennet P. E., Burton Swanson, and G.E. Tompkins. 1976. "Characteristics of Applications Software Maintenance." UCLA Graduate School of Management. This was the basis for an article that was later published in *Communications of the ACM* in June 1978, and the material in it evolved into the most important and best-known early book on software maintenance. (It does not diminish this book's importance to say that for many years it was also just about the only maintenance book around.)

In case you're inclined to believe that this fact may have eroded somehow over time, here is a more recent source:

➡ Landsbaum, Jerome B., and Robert L. Glass. 1992. *Measuring and Motivating Maintenance Programmers.* Englewood Cliffs, NJ: Prentice-Hall.

Fact 42

Enhancement is responsible for roughly 60 percent of software mainte- nance costs. Error correction is roughly 17 percent. Therefore, software maintenance is largely about adding new capability to old software, not fixing it.

Discussion

So, roughly 60 percent of software's dollar is spent on maintenance. What do those dollars buy for us?

It turns out that there's another surprise in store for us here, one of the big-ger surprises in the software field. Fully 60 percent of the maintenance dollar is spent on modifications—changes to make the software more useful. In the soft-ware field, these are called enhancements, and most of the time they stem from new requirements (business needs)—things the software product is to do that were not considered during the original development. (Sometimes they also rep-resent requirements deferred during development to facilitate meeting cost and schedule targets.)

Remember Fact 23 about requirements instability being one of the two most important causes of software runaways? Well, this is where those unstable require-ments bite us once again. The difficulty is, when software is originally developed, the customers and future users really have only a partial vision of what that prod-uct can and will do for them. It's only after the product goes into production and the users use it for awhile that they begin to realize how much more the software product could be revised to do. And, frequently, they request that those changes be made.

Is this a problem for the software field? Well, yes. Changing existing product is always difficult, no matter how "soft" the software product really is. But, no matter how much of a problem it is, it's an important service to the users of software products. We'll return, in Fact 43, to the issue of whether this phenomenon is really a problem.

At this point, let's turn to the issue of where the remaining 40 percent of the maintenance dollar is spent, once that 60 percent is taken out for enhancements. The biggest surprise of this surprising fact is how little of the maintenance dollar is spent on fixing errors. Study after study has shown that error correction is almost down in the software life cycle noise level—only 17 percent of the maintenance dollar is spent on corrections. For all the talk of buggy software, the metrics on maintenance costs do not bear out any claims that production software is error-prone.

OK, so that's 60 + 17 = 77 percent. Where does the rest of maintenance cost go? Eighteen percent is spent on something called adaptive maintenance—making the software continue to work when its environment is changed. It's to run on a new computer or on a new operating system or to interface with new packages or to accommodate new devices, for example. Notice that this 18 percent spent on adaptation is marginally more than the 17 percent spent on correction. It really is true that software error correction lies down in the life cycle cost noise level.

Oh, and by the way, what's the remaining 5 percent of the maintenance dollar spent on? The ever-popular "other." This includes, interestingly enough, maintenance done to the software to make it more maintainable. (The old term for this was *preventive maintenance*. The term *refactoring* has recently been invented to describe this activity [Fowler 1999].)

Now, I'd like to make something out of the two 60 percent facts we've been discussing here. They constitute what I like to call the 60/60 rule of software maintenance:

The 60/60 rule: 60 percent of software's dollar is spent on maintenance, and 60 percent of that maintenance is enhancement. Enhancing old software is, therefore, a big deal.

Controversy

If the first 60 percent of the 60/60 rule is frequently forgotten, the second 60 percent is forgotten even more often. Even knowledgeable software experts talk about the excessive cost of software maintenance as if it were primarily about correcting mistakes made when the product was originally built. One leader in the field, paraphrasing a business management slogan, even spoke of "obliterating" software maintenance, as if it were a bad thing. Enhancement, we are going to see in the next fact, is a good thing. This particular 60 percent stems from what is uniquely possible in the software field—enhancing old products significantly to do new things.

Sources

The sources for Fact 41 are also the sources for this fact.

Reference

➡ Fowler, Martin. 1999. *Refactoring: Improving the Design of Existing Code.* Boston: Addison-Wesley.

Fact 43   Maintenance is a solution, not a problem.

Discussion

Oh, how I love this fact! It says so succinctly what needs to be said about the field of software maintenance. (Truth be told, I suppose this is more opinion than fact. But I hope by now the previous facts have led you to accept this one as fact as well.)

Far too many people see software maintenance as a problem, something to be diminished and perhaps even "obliterated." In saying that, they are really expressing their ignorance. The only way that software maintenance could be a problem would be if nearly all of it were about fixing errors. And we have already seen that it's not. Far from it, in fact.

Maintenance, instead, is software's unique solution to the problem "we built this thing, but now we wish we had built something a little different." In the tangible products field, this is a big dilemma. If you've ever remodeled a house, for example, you know how difficult—and unpredictable—changing a tangible product can be. (A remodeler once told me that most of his clients got divorces during the [exceedingly contentious] remodeling process. I quickly decided I wouldn't do any remodeling!) Instead, modifying software to do something different is comparatively simple. (Notice the key word *comparatively.* Making changes to software is nontrivial. It's simply easier than its tangible product alternatives.)

Controversy

The controversy about this fact is simply the culmination of the controversies about the previous two. To the extent that this issue arises at all, there is probably more disagreement about this fact (and its implications) than any other in the software field. But whereas controversy is usually about the presentation of two relatively different but potentially correct points of view on a topic, in this case the notion that maintenance in software is a problem is simply untrue. (How's that for spreading trouble on oiled waters?)

Sources

Once again, the sources for this fact are the same as the sources for Facts 41 and 42. This fact is stated more elaborately (a chapter is devoted to it) in

➤ Glass, Robert L. 1991. *Software Conflict.* Englewood Cliffs, NJ: Yourdon Press.

Fact 44

In examining the tasks of software development versus software maintenance, most of the tasks are the same—except for the additional maintenance task of "understanding the existing product." This task consumes roughly 30 percent of the total maintenance time and is the dominant maintenance activity. Thus it is possible to claim that maintenance is a more difficult task than development.

Discussion

All of that 60/60 stuff suggests that we should place more attention on the big deal of software enhancement/maintenance. Not very many practitioners or researchers have, but those who have done so have made some important contributions. The biggest contribution lies in breaking down the maintenance portion of the software life cycle into its own constituent phases. After all, it's important to know more precisely where all of those software maintenance dollars are going, from an activity point of view.

As it turns out, the phases of the software maintenance life cycle are almost exactly the same as those of the development life cycle. Analyze the requirements for the problem, be it a correction or an enhancement. Design a solution within the context of the existing product's design. Code the solution, fitting it into the existing product. Test the coded solution, being careful to make sure that not only does the new change work, but it hasn't perturbed things that used to work. Then put the revised product back into production—and into more maintenance.

But in going through that laundry list of development tasks to show that the maintenance life cycle is different only by nuances, we have glossed over something very important. That problem is embedded in the innocuous-looking phrase *design a solution within the context of the existing product's design*. That's a harder task than a cursory reading of the previous paragraph would make you think. In fact, research data tells us that understanding the existing product is the most difficult task of software maintenance.

Why? Well, in a sense the answer lies in many of our previous facts: The explosion when requirements are transformed into design (Fact 26). The fact that there is no single design solution to most problems (Fact 27). The fact that design is a complex, iterative process (Fact 28). The fact that for every 25 percent increase in problem complexity, there is a 100 percent increase in solution complexity (Fact 21). All of these facts combine to tell us that design is a difficult, intellectual, even creative (Fact 22) process. What we are talking about here is what we might call undesign—the reverse engineering of the design out of an as-built product—and it is at least as complicated as the original task of design.

There is another reason why understanding the existing product, or undesign, is difficult. The original designer created what we call a design envelope, a framework within which the problem, as it was known at development time, could be solved. But the corrections and especially the enhancements will create a new set of requirements. And those new requirements may or may not fit well into the design envelope. If they fit well, the modification task will be relatively easy. If they do not fit well, the modification task will be difficult and in some cases impossible.

Remember that the development life cycle was a 20-20-20-40 affair—20 percent requirements, 20 percent design, 20 percent coding, and 40 percent error removal. Although similar, the maintenance life cycle is different in one major way. Here is the maintenance life cycle according to Fjelsted and Hamlen (1979):

- Defining and understanding the change—15 percent
- Reviewing the documentation for the product—5 percent
- Tracing logic—25 percent
- Implementing the change—20 percent
- Testing and debugging—30 percent
- Updating the documentation—5 percent

Now, let's correlate those tasks with the development life cycle:

- Defining and understanding (15 percent) is analogous to defining the requirements (20 percent)
- Reviewing and tracing (30 percent) is undesign, analogous to design (20 percent)
- Implementing (20 percent) is analogous to coding (20 percent)
- Testing and debugging (30 percent) is analogous to error removal (40 percent)
- Updating the documentation (5 percent) is not typically recorded as a separate task during development

Note that although testing and debugging consumes a large part of the maintenance life cycle (as it does during development), the new phase on the block here is undesign." It consumes 30 percent of the maintenance life cycle and thus is (tied for) the most important phase of the maintenance cycle. And it is, of course, a totally different activity from the original design activity.

Do others support this notion of the difficulty of undesign? In a survey of Air Force sites in 1983, researchers found that the "biggest problem of software maintenance" was "high [staff] turnover," at 8.7 (on a scale of 10). Close behind that, in second and third places, were "understanding and the lack of documentation," at 7.5, and "determining the place to make a change," at 6.9. A maintenance pioneer, Ned Chapin, said (also in 1983) that "comprehension is the most important factor in doing maintenance." Although these findings are fairly old, there is no reason to believe that these facts would have changed in the intervening years.

It is common, in the software world, to believe that software maintenance is something of an unworthy activity, in some way beneath the talents of the software developer. I hope this data will convince you that such is not the case. Maintenance is, in fact, quite complicated work. Unworthiness is the wrong kind of belief to attach to maintenance. It *is* hard and grubby work in that it involves delving into the high-tech innards of someone else's development activities. In that sense, it is work that not every software developer will enjoy. But it is not an unworthy activity, by any means.

Notice the small percentages in the maintenance life cycle devoted to documentation activities. The maintainer spends 5 percent of his or her time "reviewing documentation" and another 5 percent "updating documentation." If you thought about those numbers at all, you may have been surprised at how small they were. After all, if undesign is the dominant activity of maintenance, then isn't coming to understand the design through reading the product's design or maintenance documentation one of the most vital tasks? If you thought that, you would be right. Except . . .

It is important to say here that maintenance is one of those underrespected tasks of software work. Whether that lack of respect comes from its "unworthiness" or its complexity is for you to decide. But one of the things that lack of respect leads to is an almost total lack of what we might call maintenance documentation. Common sense would tell you that the design documentation, produced as the product is being built, would be an important basis for those undesign tasks. But common sense, in this case, would be wrong. As the product is built, the as-built program veers more and more away from the original design specifications. Ongoing maintenance drives the specs and the product even further apart. The fact of the matter is, design documentation is almost completely untrustworthy when it comes to maintaining a software product. The result is, almost all of that undesign work involves the reading of code (which is invariably up to date) and ignoring the documentation (which commonly is not).

Then what about "updating documentation"? There's an analogous problem. If the documentation wasn't trustworthy in the first place, most people reason, why bother to update it? Never mind that those who know about these things, such as Wiegers (2001), counter that with "don't dig the hole you're in any deeper." Here again, the underlying problem is our old enemy schedule pressure. There is too much demand for the modified product to be ready (and to be further modified with the next enhancement on the typically large backlog) for the maintainer to spend any time on fixing the documentation.

The result of all of this is that maintenance documentation is probably the least well-supported portion of the software product. In fact, if you look at the deliverables list for a typical software project, maintenance documentation is probably not even listed, nor is any provision made for updating the early life cycle documents, such as design.

Perhaps it's a stretch, but I like to tell people that, because of all of the above, maintenance is a more difficult task than software development. Few people want to hear that, so I tend to say it in something of a whisper.

But there is one person who said something similar to this who might be worth listening to. Reflecting on his efforts to learn how to program well, this person said, "[T]he best way to prepare [to be a programmer] is to write programs and to study great programs that other people have written. . . . I went to the garbage cans at the Computer Science Center and I fished out listings of their operating systems." And who was this believer in the importance of coming to understand the programs of others? You may have heard of him. His name is Bill Gates. This book is one you might enjoy because it is about how some pioneering programmers perceived their work.

Controversy

No one who has ever engaged in significant software maintenance would find this fact controversial. But there is so little interest in the maintenance portion of the software life cycle that I suspect hardly anyone has ever heard of, let alone formed an opinion on, the maintenance life cycle. Therefore there is very little controversy over this fact, although there might be considerable disbelief.

Source

The data on the software maintenance life cycle comes from an early (20-something years ago) study at one of the IBM research labs, published in the proceedings of Guide, an IBM user group conference. I am not aware of any researchers who have revisited this topic since then.

Some thoughts on software maintenance documentation can be found in places like Wiegers, listed in the following References section.

References

➡ Fjelsted, Robert K., and William T. Hamlen. 1979. "Application Program Maintenance Study Report to Our Respondents." Proceedings of Guide 48, The Guide Corporation, Philadelphia.

➡ Glass, Robert L. 1981. "Documenting for Software Maintenance: We're Doing It Wrong." In *Software Soliloquies,* Computing Trends.

➡ Lammers, Susan. 1986. *Programmers at Work.* Redmond, WA: Microsoft Press.

➡ Wiegers, Karl E. 2001. "Requirements When the Field Isn't Green." *Software Test and Quality Engineering,* May.

Fact 45   Better software engineering development leads to *more* maintenance, not less.

Discussion

Let's end the topic of software maintenance with probably the most surprising fact in a series of surprising facts. This one came as a surprise even to me when I first heard it. And, in fact, it came as a surprise to the researcher who discovered it! The study (Dekleva 1992) looked at the effect of using "modern development methods" on software projects from the point of view of their subsequent maintenance.

What were those "modern development methods"? Things like structured- or process-oriented software engineering, data-oriented information engineering, prototyping, and CASE tools—in other words, a fairly typical collection of methods, methodologies, and tools and techniques. Some of the findings were, in fact, predictable. Systems built using these approaches were more reliable than those built using older ways. They required repair less often. But those systems required more time to maintain them. How could that be?

Dekleva struggled with that issue for awhile and finally came up with what was, in retrospect, the obvious answer. These systems took longer to maintain than the others because more modifications were being made to them. And more modifications were being made because it was *easier* to enhance these better-built systems. Most organizations have a long backlog of enhancements to be made to their software products (*Software* 1988). The better-built systems were simply making their way through those enhancement queues faster than their more poorly built brethren.

This is an interesting example of the "maintenance is a solution, not a problem" phenomenon (Fact 43). If we see maintenance activities as a solution, then the more of them we perform, the better off we are. But if we're stuck seeing maintenance as a problem, there is no way we could ever see the increase in maintenance activity as a good thing.

Controversy

Few people are aware of this fact. If they were, it would be enormously controversial. If nothing else, the counterintuitive nature of the fact begs controversy. Such controversy could be extremely healthy for the software field since it would force an exploration of some of its important truths.

Sources

The sources for this fact are listed in the References section that follows.

Reference

➡ Dekleva, Sasa M. 1992. "The Influence of the Information System Development Approach on Maintenance." *Management Information Systems Quarterly,* Sept.

➡ *Software.* 1988 (Jan.). This issue of *Software* magazine (now defunct) listed the backlog of maintenance activities as 19 months for PC programs, 26 months for minicomputers, and 46 months for mainframes. Although this is clearly dated, I know of no more recent data.

CHAPTER 3

About Quality

Quality is an elusive term. And it is especially elusive in the software field. The elusiveness of the term is the primary focus of that wonderful book *Zen and the Art of Motorcycle Maintenance* (Pirsig 1974). The main character of the book, an academic looking into the real meaning of the word, went mad seeking a workable definition!

No matter how smugly we look at that madness—certainly none of *us* would ever go mad about this—the fact of the matter is that we in software have done very little better. Oh, we do an "I'll know it when I see it" kind of thing about quality. But the fact is, we neither agree on a workable definition nor agree on whose responsibility quality in the software product is. And even if we could agree on a definition, we have yet to figure out how to measure how much quality we have achieved in any given software product. Let's take each of these considerations in turn.

No workable definition? There is enormous disagreement in the field about what quality is. Worse yet, there are people in the field who believe there is no disagreement but who, in fact, are supporting a definition that is flat wrong. In this book, I present the definition that I prefer in Fact 46 (quality is a set of seven attributes) and then list the definitions that I feel are wrong in Fact 47. Warning: You may not agree with my positions on this.

Whose responsibility is quality? Most of the books and courses on software quality take the position that achieving quality is a management task. But if you could peek ahead at my definition of quality, one based on the attributes that make up quality, you would find some highly technical things. Modifiability, one of those attributes, is a matter of knowing how to build software in such a way that it can be easily modified. Reliability is about building software in ways that minimize the chance of it containing errors and then following that up with an error removal process that uses as many of the multifaceted error removal options as makes sense. Portability is about building software that can easily be moved from one platform to another. These and all the other "-ilities" of quality are deeply technical—they require a heavy dose of technical knowledge to carry off successfully. I would assert that, because of all of this, quality is one of the most deeply technical issues in the software field. Management's job, far from taking responsibility for achieving quality, is to facilitate and enable technical people and then get out of their way.

Why can't we measure quality? Because not only is quality itself elusive, but those attributes from Fact 46 that make it up are all too elusive, too. It is nearly impossible to put a number on understandability or modifiability or testability or most of the other quality -ilities. The fact that we *can* put numbers to reliability, and to some extent efficiency, does not change the fact that the slope leading to measurable quality is pretty slippery. Some years ago, the U.S. Department of Defense funded a study of measuring the -ilities (Bowen, Wigle, and Tsai 1985). The resulting three-volume report contained a lot of worksheets to be filled out (they took 4 to 25 hours apiece) and checklists to be followed. Unfortunately, when the smoke of doing all of that had cleared away, you weren't much closer to quantifying quality than you were when you started the exercise.

So, where are we going in this material on quality?

- I try to set the record right on what quality is and what it isn't.

- I take an overview of some aspects of reliability, like the characteristics of errors and their makers. In particular, I revisit some spin-offs from the earlier facts about the error removal phase of the life cycle, raising some of those spin-offs to the level of facts in their own right.

- I take an overview of some aspects of efficiency. When efficiency is important, we will see in the facts that follow, it is *really* important. There are some decades-old lessons about efficiency that deserve to be raised to the level of facts here.

- You sharp-eyed readers may note that, of the seven -ilities, I have split out only two of them (reliability and efficiency) for further emphasis. That should not lessen your view of those other -ilities. It's just that there are significant facts about these two that are both fundamentally important and oft-forgotten (that is, after all, the theme of this book).

Sources

In addition to the two sources listed in the References section that follows, see

➠ Glass, Robert L. 1992. *Building Quality Software*. Englewood Cliffs, NJ: Prentice-Hall. In Section 3.9.1, State of the Theory, this book is an analysis of the DoD report discussed earlier.

References

➠ Bowen, Thomas P., Gary B. Wigle, and Jay T. Tsai. 1985. "Specifications of Software Quality Metrics." RADC-TR-85-37, Feb.

➠ Pirsig, Robert M. 1974. *Zen and the Art of Motorcycle Maintenance*. New York: Morrow.

QUALITY

Fact 46   Quality is a collection of attributes.

Discussion

There are a lot of different ways of defining software quality. Here I want to present the definition that's stood the longest test of time.

Quality in the software field is about a collection of seven attributes that a quality software product should have: portability, reliability, efficiency, usability (human engineering), testability, understandability, and modifiability. Various software people provide somewhat different sets of names for those attributes, but this list is pretty generally accepted and has been for almost 30-something years.

What are those attributes about?

1. Portability is about creating a software product that is easily moved to another platform.

2. Reliability is about a software product that does what it's supposed to do, dependably.

3. Efficiency is about a software product that economizes on both running time and space consumption.

4. Human engineering (also known as usability) is about a software product that is easy and comfortable to use.

5. Testability is about a software product that is easy to test.

6. Understandability is about a software product that is easy for a maintainer to comprehend.

7. Modifiability is about a software product that is easy for a maintainer to change.

I have not presented these quality attributes in any kind of prioritized order. In fact, it is not possible to do that in any meaningful way. That is, there is no general, correct order in which one should try to achieve the software quality attributes. However, that is not to say that the attributes should not be ordered. For any one project, it is vitally important to establish a prioritized list of these attributes from the outset. For example, if a product is to be built for a marketplace in which it is to run on many platforms, then portability should be at or near the top of the list. If lives depend on the successful operation of a software-controlled product, then reliability must be at the top of the list. If a product is expected to have a long, useful life, then quite likely the maintenance attributes—understandability and modifiability—need to be at or near the top of the list (it is interesting to note that two of these seven attributes are explicitly about maintenance). If a product runs in a resource-starved environment, then efficiency likely belongs at the top of the list.

For example, a common prioritizing for an average project could be as follows:

1. Reliability (if a product doesn't work right, it doesn't matter much about the other attributes)

2. Human engineering (the heavy emphasis on GUIs these days speaks volumes about the importance of usability)

3. Understandability and modifiability (any product worth its software salt is probably going to be maintained for a long period of time)

4. Efficiency (I'm a little embarrassed at how low I've placed this; for some applications, this will be number 1)

5. Testability (coming in next to last doesn't diminish the importance of the attribute that can lead us most directly to reliability, which I have placed at number 1)

6. Portability (for many products, portability doesn't matter at all; for others, it probably belongs at the top of the list)

Don't be surprised if my sample ordering doesn't match yours. When I first wrote my book on software quality (Glass 1992), one of the reviewers for that book kept trying to change the (arbitrary) ordering I had used; he wanted it to match his own prioritized set of beliefs (which, incidentally, was very different from my own). I think trying to make a generalized ordering of the quality -ilities is something like creating a good software design: If any two software people agree, they probably constitute a majority.

Controversy

There are several controversies about this fact, emerging from the following questions:

1. Is this the right definition of quality?

2. Is this the right list of attributes?

3. Is there a correct ordering of these attributes?

With respect to controversy 1, there are many software folks (including some experts) in the "this is the wrong definition" camp. Most of those people use a definition among the ones I present in Fact 47. When I discuss that fact, I will tell you why I think these people are simply wrong.

With respect to controversy 2, there are software folks who take issue with the attributes in my list. One software expert, for example, argues strongly against the inclusion of portability on the grounds that if you look at the attributes of quality in other product fields, this one isn't among them. That's an interesting and, I would assert, erroneous argument. Quality attributes shouldn't be expected to be field-independent any more than their ordering should be project-independent. For example, an important quality attribute for automobiles is "fit and finish."

There are many products, including software, for which that has no meaning. There are other people who simply offer different names for the attributes in the list I have provided. On that matter, I feel much less strongly. I don't care what you call these things, as long as the concepts they represent are included in your definition of software quality.

With respect to controversy 3, we have already discussed that. There is no correct, generalized ordering, I would assert, and arguing about one is vaguely reminiscent of arguing about how many angels can dance on the head of a pin.

 ## Sources

The earliest and best known instance of this particular attribute-based definition of the quality attributes is found in the work of Barry Boehm.

➥ Boehm, Barry W., et al. 1978. *Characteristics of Software Quality.* Amsterdam: North-Holland.

My favorite elaboration on Boehm's work is found in the work cited in the Reference section that follows. An even (slightly) earlier instance of an attribute-based definition of quality is found in

➥ McCall, J., P. Richards, and G. Walters. 1977. "Factors in Software Quality." NTIS AD-A049-015, 015, 055, Nov.

 ## Reference

➥ Glass, Robert L. 1992. *Building Quality Software.* Englewood Cliffs, NJ: Prentice-Hall.

Fact 47   **Quality *is not* user satisfaction, meeting requirements, meeting cost and schedule targets, or reliability.**

 ## Discussion

So many different definitions are offered for the meaning of the word *quality* in *software quality,* that sometimes I despair. The reason I despair is that so many of those alternative definitions are clearly wrong, but their advocates clearly believe they are right.

This fact lists four of those alternate definitions. Each of them is quite appealing; each is about something important to the software field. But none of them, I would assert, is a correct definition of quality.

For a long time, I believed that something was wrong with those other definitions, but I couldn't put my finger on what that was. It wasn't until I heard a speaker from Computer Sciences Corp. provide what he called the relationship between all of these terms that I was able to point to something that clearly demonstrated that those other definitions were wrong. Here is the relationship that speaker provided:

User satisfaction = Meets requirements + delivered when needed
+ appropriate cost + quality product

This is a nicely intuitive definition of user satisfaction. A user will be satisfied if he gets a product that meets needs, is available at an appropriate time, doesn't cost a fortune, and is of reasonable quality. But what it shows, if you analyze it properly, is that all of the important entities in the relationship are distinguishable from one another. Note that one of those entities is quality. That says, I would strongly assert, that quality is clearly different from all of those other things.

Note that all of these entities are really important ones. Saying that quality is not the same as these other entities does not diminish their importance. It merely says that quality is about something else entirely. Meeting requirements and achieving schedule and cost targets are vitally important, but they are not about quality. User satisfaction is about quality, but it is also about some other pretty important things as well.

That takes care of most of the things that quality is not, in this fact. One remains, however—reliability. Many software experts equate software quality to the existence, or lack thereof, of errors in the software product. But, as we can see from Fact 46, quality is certainly about errors—that's what "reliability" is all about—but it's also about so much more.

Those experts who equate quality with lack of errors often know better. Right after a discussion in which they acknowledge all of the other attributes of quality, you may find them proceeding to discuss errors as if that were the only thing quality is about. Equating quality to reliability is seductive, since reliability is such an important focus of software quality (I grudgingly put it at number 1 in Fact 46), but doing so neglects some pretty darned important other attributes.

Controversy

This fact is a controversy all by itself! You will continue to hear people discuss quality as if it were user satisfaction or meeting requirements or achieving estimates (how that one, which I believe has nothing whatsoever to do with quality, ever got into this list, I have no idea) or being reliable. And those discussions will be supported by intense conviction. That does not diminish the fact that they are wrong.

Source

I prefer not to provide sources for these alternate and erroneous views of software quality since (a) in doing so I would be reinforcing those erroneous beliefs, and (b) I would have to confront the beliefs of some people whose names you would likely recognize. The important thing here is for all of us to accept the correct definition of quality and leave the erroneous ones behind. Until we do that, it will be difficult to discuss the subject of software quality in any meaningful way.

RELIABILITY

> **Fact 48**　　There are errors that most programmers tend to make.

Discussion

It should probably come as no surprise that some kinds of software errors are more common than others. Anyone who has ever participated in a code inspection will probably remember someone saying something like, "oh-oh, it's another one of those (brand-X) errors." The fact of the matter is, human beings are susceptible to doing certain kinds of things wrong. Off-by-one indexing. Definition/reference inconsistency. Omitting deep design details. Failing to initialize a commonly used variable. Neglecting one condition in a set of conditions.

What is odd is that few researchers have explored this matter. My source for this particular fact, in addition to my own experiences, is a paper published by a German researcher that was presented at, and published in the proceedings of, a little-known conference in Bremerhaven, Germany (Gramms 1987). That researcher called these errors "biased errors" and said they resulted from "thinking traps." This is odd because you would think that these biased errors would be among the ones that error removal techniques would focus on. Inspections, for example, could include them in their checklists. Tools to isolate and identify them could be built. Tests would be set up explicitly to trap them. Researchers could study additional ways of avoiding or detecting them.

There is another interesting facet of these biased or common errors. Among the concepts included in fault-tolerant programming (building software that tries to trap its own errors as they occur) is something called N-version programming. N-version is based on the idea that N diverse solutions to a problem from N separate teams of programmers will be unlikely to replicate the same errors; these diverse solutions, operating in conjunction with one another, could identify and vote out as erroneous any results from one solution that did not match the results of the others. But the fact of biased errors suggests that more than one of those N versions might indeed contain the same error, thus negating some of the power of the N-version approach. (This is a problem to those software development communities in which ultrareliable solutions to critical problems are essential—aerospace and rail systems, for example.)

Controversy

Although the phenomenon inherent in this fact would surprise few in the software field, it is little acknowledged—and therefore not the cause of any controversy.

Source

I know only about the German Computing Society conference (cited in the Reference section that follows) because I spoke at that same conference. My own presentation, into which I incorporated some of Gramms's findings, was

➡ Glass, Robert L. 1991. "Some Thoughts on Software Errors." In *Software Conflict*. Englewood Cliffs, NJ: Yourdon Press. Reprinted from the notes used to make the German Computing Society presentation mentioned previously.

Reference

➡ Gramms, Timm. 1987. Paper presented on "biased errors" and "thinking traps." Notices of the German Computing Society Technical Interest Group on Fault-Tolerant Computing Systems, Bremerhaven, West Germany, Dec.

Fact 49   **Errors tend to cluster.**

 ### Discussion

Try on for size this collection of statements about where software errors are found.

- "Half the errors are found in 15% of the modules" (Davis 1995, quoting Endres 1975).

- 80% of all errors are found in just 2% (sic) of the modules" (Davis 1995, quoting Weinberg 1992). Given the quote that follows, it makes you wonder if 2 percent was a misprint.)

- "About 80% of the defects come from 20% of the modules, and about half the modules are error free" (Boehm and Basili 2001).

Whatever the actual numbers, it is obvious that errors tend to be found in clusters in software products. Note that people have known this fact for several decades—the Endres quote is from 1975.

Why would this clustering of errors be so? Could it be that some parts of a program are considerably more complex than others and that complexity leads to errors? (That's my belief.) Could it be that the coding of programs is often divided up among programmers, and some programmers tend to make more errors, or discover fewer of them, than others? (That's certainly possible, given the individual differences we mentioned in Fact 2.)

What's the message of this particular fact? If you find a larger than expected number of errors in some program module, keep looking. There are quite likely to be even more there.

Controversy

The data here is sufficiently clear and of sufficient long standing that there is no controversy over this fact that I am aware of.

Sources

The sources supporting this fact are listed in the References section that follows.

References

➥ Boehm, Barry, and Victor R. Basili. 2001. "Software Defect Reduction Top 10 List." *IEEE Computer,* Jan.

➥ Davis, Alan M. 1995. *201 Principles of Software Development.* New York: McGraw-Hill. Principle 114.

➥ Endres, A. 1975. "An Analysis of Errors and Their Causes in System Programs." *IEEE Transactions on Software Engineering,* June.

➥ Weinberg, Gerald. 1992. *Quality Software Management: Systems Thinking.* Vol. 1, section 13.2.3. New York: Dorset House.

Fact 50   There is no single best approach to software error removal.

Discussion

Talk about getting redundant! I made this point several times, several facts ago. The reason I repeat it here is that it deserves to be a fact all its own, not a part of some other fact.

What's the underlying meaning of this fact? That there is no error removal silver bullet. That there is unlikely ever to be one. That testing, of whatever flavors, is not enough. That inspection and review, no matter whose definition, is not enough. That proof of correctness, if you believe in that sort of thing, is not enough. That fault tolerance, for all its value in critical software, is not enough. That whatever your favorite error removal technique, that's not enough either.

Controversy

The controversy here comes largely from the hypesters. The advocates of silver bullets will continue to make exaggerated claims for whatever technique they are selling, including error removal approaches. The fact that these advocates are consistently wrong will not keep them from stirring up these same fires in the future.

Source

This fact is one of the main themes of

➥ Glass, Robert L. 1992. *Building Quality Software.* Englewood Cliffs, NJ: Prentice-Hall.

Fact 51   Residual errors will always persist. The goal should be to minimize or eliminate severe errors.

Discussion

More redundancy! But, once again, I repeat this fact because its deserves to be a fact of its own, not piggybacking on other facts that lead us to this one.

There will always be residual defects in software, after even the most rigorous of error removal processes. The goal is to minimize the number and especially the severity of those residual defects.

When the subject of software errors arises, it is vitally important to introduce into that discussion the notion of error severity. Severe errors must be eliminated from software products. It would be nice to remove all those other errors too (for example, documentation errors, redundant code errors, unreachable path errors, errors in numerically insignificant portions of an algorithm, and so on.), but it's not always necessary.

Controversy

There is no controversy about whether there are common residual errors in software products. But there is huge controversy about whether that must remain true. Realists (some would call them pessimists or even apologists) believe that the situation won't change (because of all that complexity stuff we've been talking about). Optimists (some would call them dreamers or even advocates) believe that error-free software is within our grasp, given a sufficiently disciplined process.

One recent study (Smidts, Huang, and Widmaier 2002) casts important light on this issue. Two practitioner teams using very different software development approaches (one traditional, at CMM level 4, and one avant garde, using formal methods) were unable to build a fairly simple product that met a required goal of 98 percent reliability (even though both teams worked to "generous" cost and schedule constraints).

By now, you have probably made your own choice as to which side of this controversy you are on. I won't belabor the point further.

Source

This fact is another of the main themes of

➥ Glass, Robert L. 1992. *Building Quality Software.* Englewood Cliffs, NJ: Prentice-Hall.

Following are some interesting quotes that touch on this matter. About residual errors:

- "Disciplined personal practices can reduce defect introduction by up to 75%" (Boehm and Basili 2001).
- "About 40-50% of user programs contain non-trivial defects" (Boehm and Basili 2001). (Note that this quote is also about defect severity.)
- "You will not find all the bugs" (Kaner, Bach, and Pettichord 2002).

About severity:

- "Almost 90% of the downtime comes from, at most, 10% of the defects" (Boehm and Basili 2001).

References

➥ Boehm, Barry, and Victor R. Basili. 2001. "Software Defect Reduction Top 10 List." *IEEE Computer*, Jan.

➥ Kaner, Cam, James Bach, and Bret Pettichord. 2002. *Lessons Learned in Software Testing.* Lessons 9, 10. New York: John Wiley & Sons.

➥ Smidts, Carol, Xin Huang, and James C. Widmaier. 2002. "Producing Reliable Software: An Experiment." *Journal of Systems and Software*, Apr.

EFFICIENCY

Fact 52   Efficiency stems more from good design than from good coding.

Discussion

Ever-optimistic programmers have generally believed, over the years, that they can code their way to an efficient product. That's why assembler language, for example, has persisted so long in the history of the field. We deal with the issue of assembler language in Fact 53. Here, I want to gore the sacred cow of code over design.

For this fact to make sense, you have to think about where inefficiency comes from in the typical software product. Among other places, inefficiency emerges from external input/output (I/O) (for example, slow data accesses), clumsy interfaces (for example, unnecessary or remote procedure calls), and internal time wastage (for example, logic loops going nowhere).

Let's tackle I/O inefficiencies first. Computers are infinitely slower in fetching and replacing data on external devices than on anything else they do. Thus a penny saved in designing I/O manipulation is a dollar earned in application speed-up. There are lots of data format choices, and which you choose determines the efficiency of the resulting program more than any other choice you make. I used to try to convince academic computer scientists that the main reason for their bread and butter courses in data and file structures is to learn about which of those approaches are most efficient for which kinds of applications. After all, given the simplicity of sequential and even hashed data structures, why would anyone have ever invented linked lists and trees and indexing and the like? And why would we have data caching, a logic inefficiency solely introduced for increasing data efficiency? Because, I would tell them, data structures represent a tradeoff between increasing data structure logic complexity and improving the efficiency of data access. (Some computer scientists, convinced that efficiency is yesterday's problem, see data structures as being about interesting options for data arrangement and nothing more.)

So at design time we go to great lengths to choose just the right data structure. Or file structure. Or database approach. Why waste a lot of energy prematurely coding an inappropriate data access scheme?

Interface and internal inefficiencies pale to insignificance compared to I/O inefficiencies. Still, it is possible, through poorly designed looping strategies, for a coder to make a program's logic wheels spin an inordinately long time. (There are even "infinite loops" that never end.) Perhaps the worst offender is mathematical iterative algorithmic approaches. Slow or nonexistent algorithmic convergence can waste whole bunches of computer time. Close behind is inefficient data structure access (data does not have to be on external storage for its access to be problematic.) Once again, a little design time consideration of an efficient algorithm can be far more effective than a slickly efficient coding solution.

So what's the bottom line here? If there is a need for efficiency in a project, it must be considered early in the life cycle—well, prior to the beginning of coding.

Controversy

To some eager programmers, coding is the most important task of software construction, and the sooner we get to it, the better. Design, to people in that camp, is simply something that puts off the ultimate problem solution activity.

As long as these people continue to address relatively simple problems, (a) they will probably never be convinced otherwise, and (b) there may be nothing terribly wrong with what they are doing. But it doesn't take much problem complexity before that minimal-design, quick-to-code approach begins to fall apart. (Recall Fact 21, about how quickly problem complexity drives up solution complexity?)

What I am saying is that most of the controversy about this particular fact is between those who see design as being of little value and those who see it as an essential prelude to coding. The Extreme Programming movement, which advocates simple design approaches that evolve quickly into coding, is undoubtedly refueling this particular controversy. So is Extreme Programming's emphasis on ongoing "refactoring" to fix inefficiencies and errors in the design after it is coded.

 ## Sources

This is another one of those facts that has been known for so long that it is nearly impossible to trace it back to some kind of published roots. Any software engineering textbook (and those have been around now for 30-something years) will make this point.

To understand the argument for rushing design to get to code and refactoring it later to repair errors made in that rush to code, see the following Extreme Programming literature:

➥ Beck, Kent. 2000. *eXtreme Programming Explained.* Boston: Addison-Wesley. See the material on "simple design" and "refactoring."

The most thorough discussion of refactoring can be found in

➥ Fowler, Martin. 1999. *Refactoring: Improving the Design of Existing Code.* Reading, MA: Addison-Wesley.

Fact 53	High-order language (HOL) code, with appropriate compiler optimizations, can be about 90 percent as efficient as the comparable assembler code. Or even higher, for some complex modern architectures.

 ## Discussion

The debate about high-order language (HOL) versus assembler language is ages old in the computing field. Devotees of each have been known to go to extreme lengths to try to get their point of view to prevail on a particular project. The data needed to settle that debate has been known almost as long. The sources that follow include studies dating back to the 1970s. So although the HOL versus assembler debate feels as fresh as the edutainment application domain, where today's most die-hard assembler supporters seem to reside, the wisdom of the software ages is probably sufficient to make that debate go away.

The definitive data emerged from a flurry of studies conducted in the mid-1970s. The reason for that flurry was that the debate had become a critical issue in an emerging application domain, Avionics software (software to control the electronics of air- and spacecraft). And the findings of that flurry, nicely summarized in Rubey (1978), were "The reported . . . inefficiency of HOLs in avionics applications has been between 10 and 20% in nearly all reports." (That study went on to note that optimizations provided by optimizing compilers could add at least 10 percent to code efficiencies and that tweaking an HOL program after it is written, which is easy compared to tweaking assembler language, can add another 2 to 5 percent.)

So why has the debate raged on throughout the intervening decades? Because, in spite of that data and because of the undoubted advantages of HOL for most coding, there are times when assembler really is the better choice. In other words, the advantages of HOL are highly task-dependent; some tasks are much harder to code efficiently in HOL than others.

What are the HOL advantages? Today, naming them seems almost unnecessary since they are generally known and accepted, but here goes anyway.

- It takes far fewer lines of HOL than assembler code to solve a problem; thus productivity is dramatically higher.
- HOL code finesses whole error-prone areas of difficulty, such as register manipulation.
- HOL code can be portable; in general, assembler cannot.
- HOL code is more easily maintained (understood and modified).
- HOL code can be more readily tweaked to increase its efficiency where needed.
- HOL code can be written by less-skilled programmers.
- HOL compilers can optimize use of modern architectures, such as pipelined or cached.

What are the assembler advantages?

- HOL statements do not necessarily track with hardware features. Some assembler code can take advantage of what the hardware provides and be simpler than its HOL equivalent.

- Similarly, HOL can be awkward for interfacing with assembler-focused operating system features.

- Tight space and time considerations sometimes dictate the ultimate in efficient solutions.

Regarding assembler advantages, a nice study of the use of assembler in a tightly constrained application can be found in Prentiss (1977). On this project, the original solution was coded entirely in an HOL, and then—following a study of resulting efficiency problems—20 percent of it was recoded in assembler. That 80/20 ratio quite likely represents the maximum amount of assembler code that any system, even today, should need.

Controversy

Sometimes it feels as if this controversy may never go away! Assembler is sort of seductive technology—what "real programmer" doesn't want to get truly intimate with his or her computer and operating system? But, in fact, the controversy was really pretty well resolved back in the 1970s. The problem is, most of today's programmers aren't aware of yesterday's Avionics studies.

Sources

The sources used for this fact are listed in the following References section.

References

➡ Prentiss, Nelson H., Jr. 1977. "Viking Software Data." RADC-TR-77-168. Portions of this study, including those dealing with HOL versus assembler considerations, were reprinted in Robert L. Glass, *Modern Programming Practices* (Englewood Cliffs, NJ: Prentice-Hall, 1982).

➡ Rubey, Raymond. 1978. "Higher Order Languages for Avionics Software—A Survey, Summary, and Critique." Proceedings of NAECON Reprinted in Robert L. Glass, ed., *Real-Time Software* (Englewood Cliffs, NJ: Prentice-Hall, 1983). This study references the other studies about the efficiency of HOL versus assembler.

Fact 54	There are tradeoffs between size and time optimization. Often, improving one degrades the other.

 ### Discussion

Somehow it seems like anything that makes a program more time-efficient will also make it more size-efficient. But that is not true.

For example, consider something as trivial as a trigonometric function. Most trig functions are coded as algorithms; their code consumes very little space, but their iterative nature means that they will take some time to execute. An alternative way of providing trig functions is to build into the program a table of values and then simply interpolate among them to get a result. Interpolation is far faster than iteration but a table will be far larger than that iterative code. (This solution was actually employed on a space system I was involved with, where timing mattered a whole lot and size didn't.)

As another, perhaps more contemporary example, consider the Java programming system. Java code is not compiled into machine code; instead, it is represented in the computer as something called byte code. Byte code is much more compact than the equivalent machine code, and, as a result, Java programs tend to be very size-efficient. But time-efficient? No way! That byte code, because it is not machine code, must be interpreted while the program is executing, and interpretation sometimes adds a factor of 100 to execution time.

Thus the search for efficiency is one of compromise. The number of time efficiencies that also result in size efficiency are few in number. (An interesting point, made by Rubey (1978) in the context of HOL efficiency studies, is that size efficiency is much more easily measured than time efficiency. The former, in general, can be measured statically, while the latter must be measured dynamically. Thus, for better or for worse, it is sometimes easier to provide size efficiency than time efficiency.)

The bottom line here? If you're seeking that quality attribute called efficiency, be sure to keep in mind what kind of efficiency you most care about.

Controversy

This is simply a seldom-articulated fact, with very little controversy attached to it. Most people who care about efficiency already know about it; those who don't, however, can make some grievous errors in failing to consider it.

Source

The source for this fact is listed in the following Reference section.

Reference

➡ Rubey, Raymond. 1978. "Higher Order Languages for Avionics Software—A Survey, Summary, and Critique." Proceedings of NAECON. Reprinted in Robert L. Glass, ed., *Real-Time Software* (Englewood Cliffs, NJ: Prentice-Hall, 1983).

CHAPTER 4

About Research

It may surprise you to find the topic of research mentioned in this book at all. After all, most of the rest of the book is about things relevant to software engineering practice. Management. The life cycle. Quality. Why would I want to spend one of my precious 55 facts on research? Because, in my humble (or not so humble) opinion, there is a problem with software engineering research as it is conducted in the twenty-first century (and dating back into the twentieth century, for that matter). Research does far less than it can—far less than it should, in fact—to help practice. And there are some things that practice deeply needs from research.

Now I realize that research does not exist solely to benefit practice. I acknowledge that it is important for research to engage in the pure pursuit of theory, unfettered by practical considerations. But there is something that practice deeply needs from theory, something it is not getting. (That reminds me of a song by a favorite duo of mine, Reilly and Maloney: "The 'I Don't Know What I Want from You, but I Ain't Gettin' It' Blues." But in this case practice *does* know what it wants and what it ain't gettin'!)

What practice needs from theory is some help in understanding which new technologies really have potential benefit to practitioners and how much that benefit might be. As things stand now, we are at the mercy of the hypesters we have talked about so much in this book in knowing the benefits of these new technologies. Worse yet, sometimes those hypesters include researchers, advocating some favorite new (or old) concept of their own.

I have long said that there is a communication chasm between theory and practice in the software field. And that chasm is at its worst when researchers advocate concepts to practitioners when even they have no idea of their real-world value.

So please, researchers, pursue all of that long-term, pure theoretic research you want to. But find a little time—and budget—for some more practical things as well.

Ah, but enough talk *about* this fact. Let's have at it.

Source

➥ Glass, Robert L. 1977. "Philosophic Failures of the Field in General." In *The Universal Elixir and Other Computing Projects Which Failed.* Computing Trends. Reprinted in 1979, 1981, and 1992.

Fact 55 Many software researchers advocate rather than investigate. As a result, (a) some advocated concepts are worth far less than their advocates believe, and (b) there is a shortage of evaluative research to help determine what the value of such concepts really is.

Discussion

There are many approaches to performing research. Research can be informational, observing phenomenon or reporting on prior literature. Research can be propositional, proposing better ways of doing things. Research can be analytical, analyzing things such as case studies or theories. Or research can be evaluative, validating methods, models, or theories (Glass 1995). And, of course, research can be a mix and match of those approaches. (Regarding setting, research can be performed by academics or in industry research organizations; here, I am speaking primarily of academic research.)

There is a problem with software research. It is rarely evaluative. In the total spectrum of kinds of research, only 14 percent of software engineering research is primarily evaluative. Computer science research is only 11 percent evaluative. By contrast, the other major computing field, Information Systems, uses evaluative research as its dominant approach, at 67 percent (Glass, Vessey, and Venkatraman 2003).

The result of this failure to evaluate is that research is not helping the field understand which approaches to building software are good ones and which are not. Given the hype in our field, this leads to some pretty ugly difficulties. The people who ought to be helping us sort out the good from the bad are simply not doing that.

I have highlighted this problem before (Glass 1999), speaking of "a few glimmers of evaluative research light in an otherwise dark universe." In that study, an informational look at the few prior evaluative research findings on new software technologies, I find no support for the hyped claims of breakthrough benefits for those technologies; but, interestingly, I do find that, in general, there is support for more modest benefits (the technologies included CASE tools, Fourth Generation Languages, object orientation, formal methods, and more).

Plenty of people in recent years have tried to call attention to this problem. Potts (1993) calls this faulty research approach "research then transfer," meaning that no evaluation is performed between proposing an approach studied in propositional research and recommending that it be transferred to practice. I have used the term "advocacy research" to apply to the same phenomenon (Glass 1994). Fenton and his colleagues (1994) speak of "science and substance," with the thought that software research lacks substance and is far from being scientific. Tichy and his colleagues (1995) examined 400 computing research papers and found that 40 to 50 percent of papers in software engineering and computer science lack any evaluative component at all. (By contrast, he notes that in the field of optical engineering and neural computation, only 12 to 14 percent of published papers lack evaluation.) In fact, these cries for improving software research can be traced back at least as far as Vessey and Weber (1984), where an analysis of the literature was performed to see if there was research support for the breakthrough benefits claimed for the structured methods. (There was not.)

The problem of hype is not limited to the relationship between vendors (who sometimes do pseudo-research to support their claims) and practitioners. All too often academic software researchers propose some new concept, make grandiose claims for it, and chide those who do not immediately transfer it to practice. Formal methods are just one case in point. Until researchers begin to commit to some kinds of evaluative research, they will mislead—and be misled—about the benefits of some of their own ideas.

Controversy

Oh, yes! There is enormous controversy about this particular fact. Many researchers will deny that there is much, if any, validity to it. They do not, they believe, advocate more than they investigate. Perhaps they do not confront the hype in our field, but they do not believe that is necessarily their job. Pursuing the point of view of this particular fact in a software researcher audience is likely to result in an extremely heated discussion. It is probably true that this is the most contentious fact in this book.

Sources

The sources for this fact are listed in the following References section.

References

➡ Fenton, Norman, Shari Lawrence Pfleeger, and Robert L. Glass. 1994. "Science and Substance: A Challenge to Software Engineers." *IEEE Software,* July.

➡ Glass, Robert L. 1999. "The Realities of Software Technology Payoffs." *Communications of the ACM,* Feb.

➡ Glass, Robert L. 1995. "A Structure-Based Critique of Contemporary Computing Research." *Journal of Systems and Software,* Jan.

➡ Glass, Robert L. 1994. "The Software-Research Crisis." *IEEE Software,* Nov.

➡ Glass, Robert L., Iris Vessey, and Ramesh Venkatraman. 2003. "A Comparative Analysis of the Research of Computer Science, Software Engineering, and Information Systems." In review.

➡ Potts, Colin. 1993 "Software Engineering Research Revisited." *IEEE Software,* Sept.

➡ Tichy, Walter F., Paul Lukowicz, Lutz Prechelt, and Ernst A. Heinz. 1995. "Experimental Evaluation in Computer Science: A Quantitative Study." *Journal of Systems and Software,* Jan.

➡ Vessey, Iris, and Ron Weber. 1984 "Research on Structured Programming: An Empirical Evaluation." *IEEE Transactions on Software Engineering,* July.

PART II

5+5 FALLACIES

Introduction

The notion of adding a few fallacies to this book kind of grew on me. I started out with the idea that in the field there were far too many fundamental facts that had been either forgotten or never learned by the people who should know them. And I wanted to contribute those facts, in some fairly succinct and accessible manner, to the field.

But as I searched for those facts and the controversies surrounding them and their sources, I kept running into what I considered fallacies. Things that many people in the software field believe that are, in my not so humble opinion, just not true. Not only things that were said in some distant past by a significant software spokesperson, but things that have been repeated frequently ever since by the camp-followers and copycats of the field, often without a whole lot of thought about how much truth they contain.

At first I found only one or two fallacies. But then there were more. Finally, I decided to cap my "few fallacies" at 10. The fact that I call this group of 10 "5+5" is simply another piece of cutesiness, like the F-word alliteration described in the Introduction to the 55 Facts. I'm sure that you, or I, could identify a lot more fallacies if we set our minds to it.

Sometimes I think I should have stopped right after thinking about introducing fallacies into the book and let the matter drop there. Presenting facts is one thing; some people may disagree with some of my facts, but they can simply ignore them. But fallacies are something else. My fallacies, after all, are some other people's facts. And people who have their facts identified as fallacies are unlikely simply to ignore that slight!

So let me offer apologies in advance to some of the people whose facts I am about to morph into fallacies:

- Tom DeMarco, who has written some of the most important material in the software field and whose "you can't control what you can't measure" has been perverted into "you can't manage what you can't measure" by his camp-followers

- Jerry Weinberg, who is also one of the greats of the software field and whose notion of "egoless programming" is such a delicious mix of fact and fallacy that I simply couldn't omit considering it a fallacy here

- Harlan Mills, who was also a significant force in the software field and whose "random testing" I skewer here in one fallacy while I laud his "reading before writing" ideas in another

- The open-source movement, whose mantra "given enough eyeballs, all bugs are shallow" is flawed on so many levels that I couldn't resist calling it a fallacy

- The few academics who do research on software maintenance (yea!) and whose understanding of the topic deeply needs a dose of reality to make their findings worthwhile

- The computer science field, which is stuck teaching writing programs before reading them, knowing that is wrong but doesn't seem to know how to fix it.

So trod carefully from here on in this book. It is some people's sacred ground we are about to enter, perhaps even your own sacred ground. Prepare to feel your blood pressure rise. If you agree with my fallacies, others may not thank you for it. And if you disagree, then you are about to feel considerable discomfort.

You have been warned! Read on.

CHAPTER 5

About Management

 ### Discussion

The purpose of this saying is to point out that measurement is invaluable to managers. Clearly, managers need to know the answer to questions such as how much, when, and how well. There is a whole software engineering subfield devoted to the topic of software metrics, and proposals of new things to count—and how to count things long understood—are rampant.

What is interesting about the field of software metrics is that it is used little in practice. In surveys of tools and techniques used by software managers, metrics generally come in close to last. There are exceptions, of course—some enterprises (for example, IBM, Motorola, and Hewlett-Packard) place heavy emphasis on metric approaches. But for the most part, metric approaches are soundly ignored. Why is that? Perhaps managers are unconvinced of the value of metrics. Perhaps some of the necessary data is too hard to collect.

But there have been lots of studies of both the value and the cost of metrics, most of which have positive findings. At NASA-Goddard, for example, studies have shown that the ongoing cost of collecting the necessary metrics should be no more than 3 percent (data collection and analysis) + 4 to 6 percent (processing and analyzing the data) = 7 to 9 percent of the total cost of the project (Rombach 1990). NASA-Goddard considers that to be a bargain, given the value of their results.

155

Some of the history of metrics approaches has been tainted, however. Originally, managers all too often collected data that didn't matter or that cost too much to obtain. Such helter-skelter metrics collection was expensive and, as it turned out, pointless. It wasn't until the notion of the GQM approach (originally proposed by Vic Basili)—establish Goals to be satisfied by the metrics, determine what Questions should be asked to meet those goals, and only then collect the Metrics needed to answer just those questions—that there began to be some rationality in metrics approaches.

There was also the problem of software science. Software science was an attempt by the brilliant computing pioneer Murray Halstead to establish an underlying science for software engineering (Halstead 1977). He defined factors to measure and ways of measuring them. It seemed a worthy and, at the time, an important goal. But study after study of the numbers obtained showed neutral or negative value to the software science data. Some even likened software science to a form of astrology. The collection of "scientific" data about software projects eventually fell into disrepute and has, for the most part, been abandoned. Those who remember the software science debacle tend to taint all software metrics activities with the same brush.

Nevertheless, the collection of software metric data now happens often enough that there is even a "top 10" list of software metrics, the ones most commonly used in practice. To present an answer to the question "what are software metrics?" we present that list here.

Software Metrics	% Reported Using
Number of defects found after release	61
Number of changes or change requests	55
User or customer satisfaction	52
Number of defects found during development	50
Documentation completeness/accuracy	42
Time to identify/correct defects	40
Defect distribution by type/class	37
Error by major function/feature	32
Test coverage of specifications	31
Test coverage of code	31

Perhaps equally interesting is the list of the bottom 5 metrics:

Software Metrics	% Reported Using
Module/design complexity	24
Number of source lines delivered	22
Documentation size/complexity	20
Number of reused source lines	16
Number of function points	10

(This data comes from Hetzel [1993]. There is no reason to believe that the intervening years since 1993 would have changed this list a great deal, although advocates of function points claim a recent rise in their usage.)

Controversy

The problem with the saying "you can't manage what you can't measure"—what makes it a fallacy—is that we manage things we can't measure all the time. We manage cancer research. We manage software design. We manage all manner of things that are deeply intellectual, even creative, without any idea of what numbers we ought to have to guide us. Good knowledge worker managers tend to measure qualitatively, not quantitatively.

The fact that the saying is a fallacy should not cause us to reject the underlying truth of the message it brings, however. Managing in the presence of data is far better and easier than managing in its absence. In fact, it is the nature of managers—and human beings in general—to use numbers to help us understand things. We love batting and fielding and earned run averages. We love basket and rebound and assist counts and invent terms like *triple double* to accommodate combinations of them. We even invent data to cover subjects when there is no natural data, such as ice skating and diving (where judges assign scores to performances).

This is a case in which the fact is that measurement is vitally important to software management, and the fallacy lies in the somewhat-cutesy saying we use to try to capture that.

Source

The saying "you can't manage what you can't measure" appears most frequently in books and articles on software management, software risk, and (especially) software metrics. An interesting thing happened when I set out to track down where the saying originally came from. Several metrics experts said that it came from *Controlling Software Projects* (DeMarco 1998), and so I got in touch with Tom DeMarco himself. "Yes," said DeMarco, "it's the opening sentence in my book, *Controlling Software Projects.* But," he went on to say, "the saying is actually 'you can't control what you can't measure.'" Thus the fallacy version of the saying is actually a corruption of what DeMarco really said!

References

➡ DeMarco, Tom. 1998. *Controlling Software Projects: Management, Measurement, and Estimation.* Englewood Cliffs, NJ: Yourdon Press.

➡ Halstead, M.H. 1977. *Elements of Software Science.* New York: Elsevier Science.

➡ Hetzel, Bill. 1993. *Making Software Measurement Work.* Boston: QED.

➡ Rombach, H. Dieter. 1990. "Design Measurement: Some Lessons Learned." *IEEE Software,* Mar.

Fallacy 2   You can manage quality into a software product.

Discussion

This is a reprise of an idea presented previously in this book. In the section About Quality, I asked the question "whose responsibility is quality? My answer, as you may remember, was that no matter how many people believed" that management was responsible for product quality, there was too much technology to the subject of software quality to leave it up to management. I then went on at that point to say that nearly every one of the quality "-ilities" had deeply technical aspects, aspects that only a technologist could work with.

Not only is the achievement of quality a technical task, but those who believe that it is a management task often go about it in the wrong way. Over the years, managers have tried to use motivational campaigns to instill a quality viewpoint, as if the average technologist would be interested only in quality if he or she were pushed to do so. Sloganeering—"Quality Is Job One"—and methodologizing— "Total Quality Management"—seem to be management's chief approaches to achieving software product quality. Far from accepting these approaches, technologists tend to be alienated by them. And it doesn't help that the chief enemy of product quality on most software projects is schedule pressure. Management is motivating and methodologizing with one hand and applying antiquality schedule pressure with the other. It is simply not possible for those managers to have it both ways. And most technologists are smart enough to know that.

So what's the fallacy here? That quality is a management job. Management, of course, does have a vitally important role in achieving quality. They can establish a culture in which the task of achieving quality is given high priority. They can remove barriers that prevent technologists from instituting quality. They can hire quality people, by far the best way of achieving product quality. And they can get out of the way of those quality people, once the barriers are down and the culture is established, and let them do what they have wanted to do all along—build something they can be proud of.

Controversy

The controversy here is plentiful. When I learned I was to teach the course on software quality in the Software Engineering Master's degree program at Seattle University, I needed to pick a textbook. Every choice I examined was management-focused. To tell the quality story the way I believed it had to be told, I eventually wrote my own textbook for the course. To this day, most of the other books on quality are still management-focused.

Sources

➡ Glass, Robert L. 1992. *Building Quality Software.* Englewood Cliffs, NJ: Prentice-Hall. There is a parable on page 246 that personifies the problems of attempting to manage quality into software. The two last lines of the parable are

But who is looking out for product quality?
No one answered.

➡ DeMarco, Tom, and Timothy Lister. 1999. *Peopleware.* 2d ed. New York: Dorset House. These authors find management approaches to quality particularly distasteful. They describe management motivational campaigns as "those damn posters and plaques." The effect on a team of using this approach, they say, is "teamicide." They refer to these posters and plaques as "phony" and say that they "make most people's skin crawl." You get the general idea that these authors don't care for the usual management approaches for achieving quality.

PEOPLE

| Fallacy 3 | Programming can and should be egoless. |

 ## Discussion

There once was the first software engineering best-selling book. It was called *The Psychology of Computer Programming* (Weinberg 1971). There was a peculiar idea contained among the many excellent ideas of that book. It was the idea that the task of programming should be egoless. Programmers, the author said, should not invest their ego in the product they were building. There was, of course, an excellent reason for the author to take that position. Too many programmers, this author was saying, get so ego-invested in their product that they lose all objectivity. They see error reports as personal attacks. They see review sessions as threats. They see any questioning of what they have accomplished as being counterproductive.

What's the alternative to an ego-invested programmer? A team-player programmer. The team player sees the software product as a team effort and a team achievement. Error reports and reviews and questions become team inputs to help improve the product, not threatening attacks to derail progress.

It's hard to argue, at first glance, with the notion of the egoless programmer. Certainly the defensive programmer, caught up in his or her ego, is not open to the changes that he or she inevitably must make to improve the product. But after further thought, this notion begins to unravel. It is all well and good to advocate egoless programming, but the fact of the matter is that human ego is a very natural thing, and it is difficult to find people who can—or even should—divorce their ego from their work. Contemplate, for example, the notion of an egoless manager. That idea, of course, is preposterous! The ego of the typical manager is the driving force that makes him or her effective. We can no more divorce ego from the average programmer, I would assert, than we can or should divorce it from the average manager. We *can* strive, however, to keep that ego under control.

Controversy

Even Jerry Weinberg, the author of *The Psychology of Computer Programming* (1971), has revisited the notion of egoless programming in recent years because he has realized that it is controversial. He still believes in what he was trying to say in 1971; he believes that those who oppose the notion are taking it all too literally. It is hard to disagree with the good things that can emerge from separating ego and the programmer. Team approaches, in the form of reviews and inspections and the once-lauded chief programmer teams and perhaps even Extreme Programming's pair programming, are generally seen by many as better than their alternatives. And programmers really do need to be open to critique; the fact that we cannot write error-free programs, hammered home so many times in this book, means that programmers will always have to face up to their technical foibles and frailties.

But still, there must be some middle ground here. One of the reasons Communism eventually failed is that it assumed that we could all accept the philosophy "from each according to his ability, to each according to his need." The assumption that we could all subjugate our needs to those of others is about as faulty as the assumption that we can subjugate our egos for the betterment of the team. A system that works will have to acknowledge fundamental human traits and work within the bounds they create. And ego is one of those traits.

Source

Weinberg's book, listed in the following Reference section, is a classic book. Don't let my disagreement with the notion of "egoless" deter you from reading it and the many excellent subsequent books that Weinberg has written. (A Silver Anniversary edition of this book was republished by Dorset House in 1998.)

Reference

➡ Weinberg, Gerald. 1971. *The Psychology of Computer Programming.* New York: Van Nostrand Reinhold.

TOOLS AND TECHNIQUES

Fallacy 4	Tools and techniques: one size fits all.

Discussion

There are sure a lot of people in the software world who would like to believe that one size fits all. Those selling methodologies. Those defining process approaches. Those pushing tools and techniques. Those hoping to build component-based software. Those setting standards. Those doing research toward the next software engineering holy grail. Those academics who put the prefix *meta-* in front of whatever they're working on. All of them are seeking that "universal software elixir." Many of them even believe they have found it. All too many of them want to sell it to you!

But there's a problem here. Because software tackles such a diverse assortment of problems, it is becoming more and more obvious that there are few, if any, universal solution approaches. What works for business application programs will never be enough for critical, real-time software projects. What works for systems programming is often irrelevant to the needs of scientific applications. What works for small projects, and that includes today's Agile Development approaches, won't work well for those huge projects that consume hundreds of programmers. What works for straightforward projects will fail miserably if applied to critical projects.

We are just beginning, in our field, to appreciate how diverse the problems we need to solve really are. I've taken a stab at the dimensions of the problem (Glass and Oskarsson 1996).

- Size matters. Small is vastly easier than huge.

- Application domain matters. For example, what is needed for scientific applications—a strong mathematical foundation, among other things — is typically unnecessary for business and systems programs.

- Criticality matters. If lives or vast sums of money are involved in a project, you will treat it far differently—especially its reliability needs—than if they are not.

- Innovativeness matters. If the problem you are addressing is unlike any you have ever solved before, you will take a much more exploratory and much less methodologized approach to its solution.

Certainly others have their own favorite dimensions. For example, Jones (1994) divides the field of applications into Management Information Systems, Systems Software, Commercially Marketed Products, Military Software, Contract/Outsourced Software, and End-User Software (he then does a wonderful job of characterizing each of those domains, including discussions of their most common risk factors).

Probably you have your own favorite dimensions. Most practitioners are well aware that "my project is different." All too many theorists, however, disdain such a comment and see that practitioner as simply unwilling to try new (and often "universal") things (but see Glass 2002a).

Controversy

This particular fallacy is coming to a head. The many people who continue to believe in the one-size-fits-all approach are finding an ever-increasing number of opponents. Plauger (1994) says that "anyone who believes that one size fits all belongs in a pantyhose commercial." Yourdon (1995) says "the most interesting paradigm shift now taking place" in the field is "the shift away from the notion that all software is essentially the same." Sanden (1989) writes about "eclectic design approaches." Vessey and Glass (1998) point out that, in the discipline of problem solving, problem-focused solution approaches (like a specific size of wrench) are seen as "strong" and generalized ones (like a monkey wrench) as "weak." Project differences are celebrated (Glass 2002a). Even the commonly disdained notion of "ad hoc" is coming in for some reappraisal (Glass 2002b) (the dictionary says it means "fitted to the problem at hand"). If you think one-size-fits-all is a bad thing, then you will see this groundswell of opposition to the notion as one that is extremely healthy for the field.

Sources

The opposition to the notion of one-size-fits-all is taking on an accelerated drumbeat. The newly popular Agile Development approaches, for example, say things like "different methodologies are needed for different projects" and go on to speak of the "sweet spot" projects in which Agile is at its best (Cockburn 2002): two to eight people in one room, on-site usage experts, one-month project increments, experienced developers. Following through on this theme, they also note the (very different) projects where traditional/rigorous approaches are best (Highsmith 2002): larger teams, critical projects, projects involving regulatory considerations.

➥ McBreen, Pete. 2002. *Software Craftsmanship.* Boston: Addison-Wesley. Contains a section explicitly titled One Size Does Not Fit All.

References

➥ Cockburn, Alistair. 2002. *Agile Software Development.* Boston: Addison-Wesley.

➥ Glass, Robert L. 2002a. "Listen to Programmers Who Say 'But Our Project is Different.'" The Practical Programmer. *Communications of the ACM.*

➥ Glass, Robert L 2002b. "In Search of Meaning (A Tale of Two Words)." The Loyal Opposition. *IEEE Software.*

➡ Glass, Robert L., and Östen Oskarsson. 1996. *An ISO Approach to Building Quality Software.* Upper Saddle River, NJ: Prentice-Hall.

➡ Highsmith, Jim. 2002. *Agile Software Development Ecosystems.* Boston: Addison-Wesley.

➡ Jones, Capers. 1994. *Assessment and Control of Software Risks.* Englewood Cliffs, NJ: Yourdon Press.

➡ Plauger, P.J. 1994. *Programming on Purpose.* Englewood Cliffs, NJ: Prentice-Hall.

➡ Sanden, Bo. 1989. "The Case for Eclectic Design of Real-Time Software." *IEEE Transactions on Software Engineering* SE-15 (3). (The journal, not understanding the word *eclectic*, replaced it with *electric* when they published the article!)

➡ Vessey, Iris, and Robert L. Glass. 1998. "Strong vs. Weak Approaches to Systems Development." *Communications of the ACM*, Apr.

➡ Yourdon, Ed. 1995. "Pastists and Futurists: Taking Stock at Mid-Decade." *Guerrilla Programmer*, Jan.

Fallacy 5   Software needs more methodologies

Discussion

The strange thing about this fallacy is, I can't think of anyone who is actually saying it. But before you move rapidly on to the next fallacy, muttering to yourself "what is this guy up to here?" let me point out the problem. No one is talking about inventing more methodologies, but everyone seems to be doing it.

Gurus do it. Graduate students do it. Opponents of the rigorous/rigid methodologies do it. Even professors and researchers do it, on occasion. "People who want to make their mark in the [software] world invent yet another method or model," (Wiegers 1998). The methodology machine seems to be cranking quite rapidly and seemingly continuously.

There's another funny thing about this fallacy. Study after study in the methods engineering research community (Hardy, Thompson, and Edwards 1995; Vlasbom, Rijsenbrij, and Glastra 1995) has shown that almost no software practitioners are using these methodologies straight out of the box. On the contrary, most people who use a methodology adapt it to fit the situation at hand.

At first, the methods engineering folk were troubled by this fact. "How dare practitioners tinker with the wisdom of the methodologist?" they seemed to be saying. But as time passed, the methods engineering people came to grips with what was happening—methodologies were bent to fit because they needed to be bent to fit. Practitioners were exhibiting a necessary form of wisdom, not a perverse form of obstinacy.

Now, this fallacy is about whether we need all those methodologies that those methodologists are cranking out. And the fact of the matter is, many would say, we don't. One particularly vocal opponent of the creation of more methodologies, Karl Wiegers (you've heard of him before in this book), goes so far as to base keynote addresses on it. "Read my lips," the title of his presentation goes. "No new models" (by which he means "techniques, methods, and methodologies").

Why does Wiegers say that? Because, he says, no one is using the methodologies we have now. If shelfware is the current status of many software tools, then "dull thud" is the status of most methodologies. Methodologies appear on the scene, he says, and are roundly ignored by the people who are intended to be using them.

Should they be ignoring these methodologies? Ah, that's a fair question, but it's probably one for another fallacy—or fact. My personal suspicion, however, is that all too many of our methodologies have been the product of (a) ignorance (what does a graduate student or even a faculty member know about the gritty real world of software practice?) and (b) a kind of police mentality (all too many gurus seem to want people to use their methodologies because *it's the right thing to do*, not because they can demonstrate that they really help in the building of software). DeMarco and Lister (1999) point out that there are Big-M Methodologies and little-m methodologies, where the rigid big-M's come from what they might call the "methodology police." DeGrace and Stahl (1993) make the same distinction but with different terminology—"Roman" is their word for the methodology police form, and "Greek" is the name for a more flexible form. Given all of that, my personal opinion is that little-m's are good things, and big-M's are largely bad and should be used only with considerable care.

Controversy

I don't believe anyone is drawing a line in the sand about this fallacy, except Karl Wiegers. But perhaps someone should. There is plenty for us to learn about methodologies.

- Are any of them really supported by empirical evidence? (For the most part, the answer is "no.")

- Is the lack of use caused by ineffective methodologies or ignorant potential users?
- Should practitioners be bending them to fit? If so, why?
- Should methodologies be applied enterprise-wide, or is this too much one-size-fits-all?
- Should methodologies be swallowed whole, or should we use a "best of breed" selection process on their constituent elements?
- Is there a rationale behind the constituent elements of a methodology (any methodology), more than just "they seemed to fit together nicely"?
- When do we use which methodologies? Or which of their constituent elements?

My personal belief is that until we have the answer to most of these questions, we should tread carefully on this subject. That's a bit of an irony, of course, given that we have been zestfully using methodologies for several decades now (the structured methods, information engineering, object orientation, Extreme Programming, Agile approaches, and so on).

So, is there controversy? Absolutely. We have more methodologies than we know what to do with already. We have tons of unanswered questions about them. And we have people continuing to invent methodologies as if their careers depended on it. Let's call a halt to all of this. Let's get some of those questions answered. Let's listen to Karl Wiegers's cry, "No new models."

Sources

In addition to the sources listed in the Reference section that follows, the following provides a summary and interpretation of the various views on methodologies.

➡ Glass, Robert L. 1995. *Software Creativity.* Englewood Cliffs, NJ: Prentice-Hall.

References

➡ DeGrace, Peter, and Leslie Stahl. 1993. *The Olduvai Imperative: CASE and the State of Software Engineering Practice.* Englewood Cliffs, NJ: Prentice-Hall.

➡ DeMarco, Tom, and Timothy Lister. 1999. *Peopleware.* 2d ed. New York: Dorset House.

➥ Hardy, Colin J., J. Barrie Thompson, and Helen M. Edwards. 1995. "The Use, Limitations, and Customization of Structured Systems Development Methods in the United Kingdom." *Information and Software Technology,* Sept.

➥ Vlasbom, Gerjan, Daan Rijsenbrij, and Matthijs Glastra. 1995. "Flexibilization of the Methodology of System Development." *Information and Software Technology,* Nov.

➥ Wiegers, Karl. 1998. "Read My Lips: No New Models!" *IEEE Software,* Sept.

ESTIMATION

Fallacy 6	To estimate cost and schedule, first estimate lines of code.

Discussion

Estimation, we mentioned in several of the facts earlier in this book, is a vitally important activity in software. But, as we also saw in those facts, we struggle mightily to find ways to do it well.

Somehow, over the years, we have evolved—as *the most popular way of performing estimation*—the notion of first estimating the size of the product to be built in lines of code (LOC). From that, according to this idea, we can then do a conversion of LOC to cost and schedule (based, presumably, on historical data relating LOC to the cost and schedule needed to build those LOC). The idea behind the idea is that we can estimate LOC by looking at similar products we have previously built and extrapolating that known LOC data to fit the problem at hand.

So why is this method, acknowledged to be the most popular in the field, fallacious? Because there is no particular reason why the estimation of LOC is any easier or more reliable than the estimation of cost and schedule. Because it is not obvious that there is a universal conversion technique for LOC to cost and schedule (we already skewered the one-size-fits-all notion in the previous fact). Because one program's LOC may be very different from another program's LOC: Is one line of COBOL code the same degree of complexity as one line of C++ code? Is one line of a deeply mathematical scientific application comparable to one line of a business system? Is one line of a junior programmer's code equivalent to one line from your best programmer? (See Fact 2 about those individual differences—up to 28 to 1—for an answer to that question.) Is one LOC in a heavily commented program comparable to a LOC in one with no comments? What, in fact, constitutes a LOC?

Controversy

Let the controversy begin!

I already came down hard on this fallacy in Fact 8, where I said "this idea would be laughable—in the sense that it is probably harder to know how many LOC a system will contain than what its schedule and cost will be—if it were not for the fact that so many otherwise bright computer scientists advocate it."

You think that was harsh? You haven't begun to experience the ferocious opposition that exists to this fallacy. Capers Jones, in most of his writings, goes absolutely ballistic about LOC approaches. In identifying the biggest risks in the software field, he places inaccurate metrics at number one and loses no time in saying that LOC metrics are the reason he chose this number one. "It was proven in 1978 that 'lines of code' . . . cannot be safely used to aggregate productivity and quality data" (Jones 1994). He goes on to list "six serious problems with LOC metrics," and later, in case you didn't connect "inaccurate metrics" specifically to LOC, he says, "The usage of LOC metrics ranks as the most serious problem."

In case that number one risk didn't sufficiently deter you from believing in LOC approaches, Jones (1994) goes on to list these additional "top 10" risks that are related in some way to the use of LOC (Jones's rankings are shown in parentheses):

- Inadequate measurement (2)
- Management malpractice (4)
- Inaccurate cost estimating (5)

It would be possible to list here some others who stir the controversy of the use of LOC in estimation. But all of them would pale to insignificance next to the vitriol of the Jones opposition!

 Source

Jones (1994), a wonderful and unique book in spite of (not because of) Jones's strident opposition to LOC, is listed in the following Reference section.

Reference

➡ Jones, Capers. 1994. *Assessment and Control of Software Risks.* Englewood Cliffs, NJ: Yourdon Press.

CHAPTER 6

About the Life Cycle

TESTING

Fallacy 7   Random test input is a good way to optimize testing.

 Discussion

In Fact 32 (the one about test coverage that says it is nearly impossible to achieve 100 percent coverage), I first brought up the notion of random testing. There I described it as one of the four basic testing approaches. Those four approaches are requirements-driven testing, structure-driven testing, statistics-driven testing, and risk-driven testing. This fallacy is about what I called, at that time, statistics-driven testing.

"Statistics-driven testing" is pretty much just a nicer way of saying random testing. It is the notion of generating test cases at random, trying to cover all of the nooks and crannies of the software not by looking at the requirements or the structure or the risks, but simply looking at random. To give that a bit more sophistication, one of the random test case approaches is to generate tests from the operational profile of the software. That is, test cases are chosen at random, but they must fit the typical usage the software will be put to.

There is one significant advantage to this kind of randomized testing. Given that all test cases will be drawn from the population that users will run, the result of randomized testing can be used to simulate real usage. In fact, via statistics-driven testing, software people can say things like "this product runs successfully 97.6 percent of the time." That's a pretty potent kind of statement to make to users. It's certainly more meaningful to those users than "this product has met 99.2 percent of its requirements" (that sounds impressive, but we already know that 100 percent requirements-driven testing is far from sufficient) or "this product has had 94.3 percent of its structure tested" (the typical user has no idea what "structure" is) or "this product has successfully passed tests covering 91 percent of the risks it is to handle" (risks about the process or risks about the product? risks that the user has provided or bought into? and is anything less than 100 percent risk testing success ever acceptable?).

But the disadvantages of randomized testing are plentiful. For one thing, it represents a crapshoot. If the tests are truly random, then the programmer or tester has no idea what parts of the software have been thoroughly tested and what parts have not. In particular, exception case handling is critical to the success of most software systems (some of the worst software disasters have been about failed exception handling), and there is no particular reason to believe that random tests will hit exception code—even (or especially) when those tests are focused on the operational profile.

For another thing, it ignores the wisdom and the intuition of the programmer and the tester. Remember that there are "biased" (common) errors that most programmers tend to make (Fact 48) and that errors tend to cluster (Fact 49). Many programmers and testers intuitively know these things and are able to focus their testing efforts on those kinds of problems. In addition, most programmers know what parts of the problem solution gave them a hard time and will focus their test efforts on them. But random testing does not "know" these things and therefore cannot focus on them (if it did, it wouldn't be truly random).

For yet another thing, there is the problem of repeat testing. Such testing approaches as regression testing, where a fixed set of tests is run against a revised version of a software product, require the same set of tests to be run repeatedly. So does the use of test managers, test tools that compare the result of this test case run with a previously successful or known-to-be-correct test "oracle." If random tests are truly random, then there is no provision in the idea for repeating the same set of tests over and over. Of course, it would be possible to generate a set of tests randomly and "freeze" them so that they could be repeated. But that brings us to the next facet of random testing, "dynamic" random testing.

Dynamic random testing is the notion that the test cases should be regenerated as testing proceeds, with a particular success criteria in mind. For example, those computer scientists who are enthusiastic about "genetic algorithms" have turned to test case generation ("genetic testing") as an application of that theory. The test cases are randomly generated to meet some sort of success criteria, and they are adjusted (dynamically changed) to improve their rating with respect to that criteria as testing proceeds. (For a better and more thorough explanation, see, for example, Michael and McGraw [2001].) But, of course, such dynamic test cases cannot be repeatable without twisting the philosophy of dynamic testing.

Controversy

What makes random testing, and the claim that its use can be optimal, most controversial is that some well-known computer scientists have advocated it as a key part of their error removal philosophies. For example, the late Harlan Mills made it part of his "Cleanroom" approach to error removal (Mills, Dyer, and Linger 1987). This in-itself controversial approach called for

- Formal verification (proof of correctness) of all code
- Programmers doing no testing at all
- An independent test group doing all testing
- All testing to be random, based on operational profiles

Cleanroom approaches to error removal are occasionally used in practice, but usually some parts of the philosophy are bent to fit the situation at hand. For example, formal verification is often replaced with rigorous inspection (we have already seen, in Fact 37, how effective that approach can be). I suspect, but I have seen no data to prove it, that the exclusive use of randomized testing is also often modified (or nullified).

Another controversy has arisen more recently. We already mentioned genetic testing (Michael and McGraw 2001). That study also performed an evaluation of random testing and concluded that it becomes less effective as the size of the software under test becomes larger:

> In our experiments, the performance of random test generation deteriorates faster than can be accounted for simply by the increased number of conditions that must be covered. This suggests that satisfying individual test requirements is harder in large programs than in small ones. Moreover, it implies that, as program complexity increases, non-random test generation techniques become increasingly desirable.

Another victim of software complexity—random test case generation—appears to be about to bite the dust. That's what makes it one of my fallacies. It may or may not survive as a testing approach, but it is extremely unlikely ever to be seen again as an optimal approach.

 ### Sources

The sources supporting this fact are listed in the following References section.

 ### References

➧ Michael, Christopher C., and Gary McGraw. 2001. "Generating Software Test Data by Evolution." *IEEE Transactions on Software Engineering,* Dec.

➧ Mills, Harlan D., Michael Dyer, and Richard Linger. 1987. "Cleanroom Software Development: An Empirical Evaluation." *IEEE Transactions on Software Engineering,* Sept.

REVIEWS

Fallacy 8	"Given enough eyeballs, all bugs are shallow."

 ### Discussion

There's a reason that this fallacy is in quotes. It's one of the mantras of the open-source community. It means, "if enough people look at your code, all of its errors will be found."

That seems innocent enough. So why have I included it as a fallacy? There are several reasons. They range from the picky

- The depth or shallowness of an error is unrelated to the number of people searching for it;

to the relevant

- Research on inspections suggests that the increase in the number of bugs found diminishes rapidly as the number of inspectors rises;

to the vital

- There is no data demonstrating that this statement is true.

Let's take each of these reasons in turn.

The picky. This is probably just wordplay. But it is patently obvious that some bugs are more shallow than others and that that depth does *not* change, no matter how many people are seeking them. The only reason for mentioning this particular reason here is that too many people treat all bugs as if their consequences were all alike, and we have already seen earlier in this book that the severity of a bug is extremely important to what we should be doing about it. Pretending that turning scads of debuggers loose will somehow reduce the impact of our bugs is misleading at best.

The relevant. This is important. The research on software inspections shows that there is a maximum number of useful inspection participants, beyond which the success of an inspection falls off rapidly (see, for example, Fact 37). And that number is quite finite—somewhere in the range of two to four. So, if that finding is valid, we must question the "given enough eyeballs" statement. Of course, the more people who join in debugging, the more bugs will be found. But we shouldn't think that a Mongolian horde of debuggers, no matter how well motivated they are, will produce an error-free software product, any more than any of our other error removal approaches will.

The vital. There is simply no evidence that the thought behind this fallacy is true. I have heard open-source zealots cite various research sources to prove that open-source software is more reliable than its alternatives (because of all those eyeballs). I have pursued each of the sources so identified and found that they do no such thing. For example, the so-called Fuzz Papers have been cited as being a research study that concludes that open-source software is more reliable (Miller). Actually, the Fuzz Papers are only marginally about open source, they use a questionable research approach, and even their author is unwilling (in a personal communication) to conclude that open-source is more reliable. (He believes that it may well be, but he says that his research sheds no light on whether it is.) In fact, Zhao and Elbaum (2000) show that open-source programmers probably use no more error removal approaches than those used by non-open source programmers, probably because they are expecting all those eyeballs to do the job for them (a dubious expectation because they do not control and cannot know how many of those eyeballs are really applied to their work).

Controversy

Tread lightly on the beliefs of vocal zealots! I do not expect that open source advocates are going to take this particular fallacy lying down!

Is there controversy? Oh, yes there is—or soon will be! One of the most important tenets of the open-source community is that their approach produces better software. And this fallacy, which in essence is saying that no one knows whether that is true, attacks the heart of that tenet.

So why have I stood up here in front of the open-source steamroller? Because it is important to get at the facts here. Because no software movement, no matter how many vocal zealots it contains, should be allowed to hype the field without challenge. And make no mistake about it—these unsubstantiated claims are just as much hype as the claims for automatic generation of code from specifications or for the programming without programmers claims made for 4GLs and CASE tools by the non-open source zealots before them.

Note that I am not saying that open-source software is less reliable than its alternatives. What I am saying is that (a) one of its mantras is a fallacy, and (b) there is little or no evidence on whether this tenet is true.

Sources

In addition to the sources listed in the following References section, see these analyses:

➥ Glass, Robert L. 2001. "The Fuzz Papers." *Software Practitioner,* Nov. Provides analysis of the content of the Fuzz Papers with respect to open-source reliability.

➥ Glass, Robert L. 2002. "Open Source Reliability—It's a Crap Shoot." *Software Practitioner,* Jan. Provides an analysis of the content of the Zhao and Elbaum study, in the following section.

References

➥ Miller, Barton P. "Fuzz Papers." There are several Fuzz Papers, published at various times and in various places, all written by Prof. Barton P. Miller of the University of Wisconsin Computer Science Department. They examine the reliability of utility programs on various operating systems, primarily UNIX and Windows (with only passing attention to Linux, for example).

The most recent Fuzz Paper as of this writing appeared in the Proceedings of the USENIX Windows Systems Symposium, Aug. 2000.

➡ Zhao, Luyin, and Sebastian Elbaum. 2000. "A Survey on Quality Related Activities in Open Source." *Software Engineering Notes,* May.

MAINTENANCE

Fallacy 9	The way to predict future maintenance costs and to make product replacement decisions is to look at past cost data.

Discussion

We humans tend to predict the future based on the past. After all, you can't exactly predict the future by looking at the future. So we assume that what is about to happen will be similar to what has already happened. Sometimes that approach works. In fact, it works fairly often. But sometimes it doesn't work at all.

A couple of interesting questions that come up fairly frequently during software maintenance are

- What's it going to cost us to keep maintaining this product?
- Is it time to consider replacing this product?

Those questions are not only interesting, they're important. So it's not surprising that our old predictive friend, "let's base our beliefs about the future on the past," raises its head in this context. The question is, does that method of prediction work for software maintenance?

To answer that, let's consider for a moment how maintenance occurs. It largely consists, as we saw in Fact 42, of enhancements. So it will do us little good to look at the repair rates of a software product. What we would need to look at, if this predictive approach is to work at all, is the enhancement rate of the product.

So, are there logical trends to enhancement rates? There's not much data to go on to answer this question, but there are some facts to be considered. Those who write about software maintenance have long said that there's a "bathtub" shape to maintenance costs (Sullivan 1989). There's a lot of maintenance when a product is first put into production because (a) the users have fresh insight into the problem they're trying to solve and discover a host of new, related problems they'd like worked, and (b) heavy initial usage tends to flush out more errors than later, more stable usage. Then time passes, and we descend into the stable, low-maintenance middle of the maintenance process; as enhancement interest drops off, the bugs are pretty well under control, and the users are busy getting value from using the product. Then, after the product has been on the air for awhile, it has been pushed through accumulated change to the ragged edge of its design envelope, the point at which simple changes or fixes tend to get much more expensive, and we reach the upward slope at the other edge of the bathtub. Changes of the kind that used to be cheap are now getting expensive.

At that point, with maintenance costs on the rise again, something a bit harder to predict happens. The increasing cost of making simple changes to the product and the increasing length of the change queue, deter users from requesting any more changes, or users simply quit using the product because they can no longer make it do what they want. Either way, maintenance costs tend to decline again, probably precipitously. The bathtub has developed a slippery right-tail slope.

Now, let's go back to the issue of predicting the future based on the past. There is a predictable shape to all of what we just finished describing, of course, but predicting the timing of those changes of shape becomes both vital and nearly impossible. Are we at the bottom of the bathtub, with costs pretty stable? Are we on our way up to the edge of the bathtub, where maintenance costs will continue to rise? Have we tipped over the edge and begun down the slippery slope, in which case maintenance costs will decline? Worst of all, are we at an inflection point, where the shape of the curve is suddenly changing? Or is this software product somehow different from the ones we have been discussing, such that there is no bathtub or slippery slope at all? These are the kinds of issues that tend to drive mathematical curve-fitters bonkers.

Based on all of this, I would assert that basing predictions of future maintenance costs on what has happened in the past is pretty fruitless: (a) It's extremely difficult to predict what future maintenance costs will be, and (b) it's also nearly impossible to predict a meaningful decision point for product replacement.

With respect to the future costs issue, it's probably better to ask the customers and users about their expectations for future change, rather than trying to extrapolate the future from past maintenance data. With respect to the product replacement issue, the news is even worse. Most companies now find that retiring an existing software product is nearly impossible. To build a replacement requires a source of the requirements that match the current version of the product, and those requirements probably don't exist anywhere. They're not in the documentation because it wasn't kept up to date. They're not to be found from the original customers or users or developers because those folks are long gone (for the average software product that has been around for a substantial period of time). They may be discernible from reverse engineering the existing product, but that's an error-prone and undesirable task that hardly anyone wants to tackle. To paraphrase an old saying, "Old software never dies, it just tends to fade away."

So, is the notion of predicting future software maintenance costs based on past costs a fallacy? You betcha! Probably more of a fallacy than you ever dreamed.

Controversy

The only reason for including this matter as a fallacy is this: Those academic researchers who look at the issue of maintenance (and all too few do) tend to want to use nice, clean, mathematical approaches to answer the kinds of questions we have been discussing here. And those researchers know almost none of the facts about the shape of the maintenance curve. So they assume that the maintenance cost for a product will continue to rise, higher and higher and faster and faster, until it becomes intolerable.

And here they make an additional mistake: They assume that it is repair costs, not enhancement costs, that they ought to be studying. That higher and higher, faster and faster curve may be unpleasant, but at least it represents a predictable shape, one you can feed into mathematical models. And that point of intolerability is the point at which you replace the product. Isn't theory wonderful? It answers questions that the messy real world has difficulty even formulating.

The first time I heard an academic present a paper on this approach at a conference, I went up to him afterwards and quietly informed him as to why his idea wouldn't work. I gave him my card and said that I would provide him with some sources of information that would explain why his ideas were wrong. He never contacted me! That author's work has instead become the research baseline on which a lot of follow-on research has been based. Other researchers reference that work as a seminal paper in the maintenance prediction world.

So I'm stating this item as a fallacy here, hoping that some of those researchers, heading pell-mell down their own mathematics-based slippery curve-fitting slope, will see this and realize the error of their ways.

Sources

I won't cite that seminal-but-wrong paper here, on the grounds that the author and his camp-followers will recognize whom I'm talking about, and no one else needs to know or will care. But here are a few other related sources about making maintenance decisions, including product replacement:

➡ Glass, Robert L. 1991. "The ReEngineering Decision: Lessons from the Best of Practice." *Software Practitioner,* May. Based on the work of Patricia L. Seymour, an independent consultant on maintenance matters, and Martha Amis of Ford Motor Co.

➡ Glass, Robert. 1991b. "DOING Re-Engineering." *Software Practitioner,* Sept.

Reference

➡ Sullivan, Daniel. 1989. Presentation by Daniel J. Sullivan of Language Technology, Inc., at the Conference on Improving Productivity in EDP System Development.

CHAPTER 7

About Education

| Fallacy 10 | You teach people how to program by showing them how to *write* programs. |

 Discussion

How did you learn to program? I'll bet it was at some sort of academic class, at which the teacher or professor showed you the rules for a programming language and turned you loose on writing some code. And if you learned to program in more than one language, I'll bet it was the same. You read or were taught about this new language, and off you went, writing code in it.

That's so much the norm in learning to program that you probably don't see anything wrong with that. But there is. Big time.

The problem is this: In learning any other language, the first thing we do is learn to *read* it. You get a copy of *Dick and Jane* or *War and Peace* or something somewhere in between, and you read. You don't expect to write your own version of *Dick and Jane* or *War and Peace* until you've read lots of other examples of what skilled writers have written. (Believe me, writing *Dick and Jane* does require skill! You have to write using a vocabulary that's age- and skill-appropriate for your readers.)

So how did we in the software field get stuck on this wrong track, the track of teaching writing before reading? I'm not really sure. But stuck on it, we are. I know of no academic institution, or even any textbook, that takes a reading-before-writing approach. In fact, the standard curricula for the various computing fields—computer science, software engineering, information systems—all include courses in writing programs and none in reading them.

Earlier I asked somewhat rhetorically how we got started so badly in this area. I do have some thoughts on the matter.

1. To teach code reading, we must select some examples of code to be read. Perhaps it is to be top-notch code. The search for such exemplars is a rocky one. Perhaps it is to be flawed code, to teach lessons on what not to do. That's a difficult search, too. The problem is, we in the software world don't always agree on what good code or bad code is. Furthermore, most programs don't consist of just good or bad code— they contain a mixture of both. The SEI conducted a search several years ago for some exemplar code for this very purpose and finally gave up. In the end, they settled for some typical code, with some good and some bad examples. (In spite of the fact that most programmers think that they're the best in the world at their craft, I think we have to admit that the *War and Peace* of software has not yet been written!)

2. To teach code reading, we need some textbooks that tell us how. There are none. Every programming textbook I know of is about writing, not reading. One of the reasons for that is that no one knows how to write a book on reading code. I recently reviewed a candidate manuscript on this subject for a leading publishing house. At first glance, it looked like we were on the way to solving this problem. But there was a serious problem with this manuscript, written by an accomplished author, that caused me (reluctantly) to recommend rejection. It was written for an audience of people who already knew how to program, and they aren't the ones who need to learn reading-before-writing. It's novices who so deeply need such a textbook (I told you that writing *Dick and Jane* required skill).

3. Many years ago, we defined standard curricula for the software-related academic disciplines, as I mentioned earlier. That was a good thing. But, in those standard curricula, not a thought was given to teaching code reading. What all of that means is that teaching writing-before-reading is now institutionalized. And you know how hard it is to change institutionalized things!

4. The only time we in software tend to read code is during maintenance. Maintenance is a much disdained activity. One of the reasons for that is that code reading is a very difficult activity. It is much more fun to write new code of your own creation than to read old code of someone else's creation.

Controversy

Almost anyone who thinks about the issue of learning to program realizes that we are going about it wrong. But hardly anyone seems to be willing to step forward and try to change things (the author of the textbook that I recommended rejecting was one of the few exceptions). There are advocates of reading-before-writing, as we will see, but nothing seems to come of that advocacy. The result is that there is no controversy on this topic, when in fact some heated controversy might be extremely healthy for the field.

Sources

If you've never thought much about this issue—and I think that's the norm for software people—you will be surprised at a representative list of those who have taken some kind of position on this matter.

➡ Corbi, T. A. 1989. "Program Understanding: Challenge for the 1990s." *IBM Systems Journal* 28, no. 2. Note the date on this paper—this is an issue that has been around for some time. The author says "For other 'language' disciplines, classical training includes learning to speak, read, and write. . . . Many computer science departments sincerely believe that they are preparing their students for the workplace. . . . Acquiring programming comprehension skills has been left largely to on-the-job training."

➡ Deimel, Lionel. 1985. "The Uses of Program Reading." *ACM SIGCSE Bulletin* 17, no. 2 (June). This paper argues that program reading is important and should be taught and suggests possible teaching approaches.

➡ Glass, Robert L. 1998. Software 2020, Computing Trends. This collection of essays contains one titled "The 'Maintenance First' Software Era," which takes the position that maintenance is a more important software activity than development and recommends the teaching of reading before writing because reading is what maintainers have to do.

➡ Mills, Harlan. 1990. Presentation at a software maintenance conference, as quoted in Glass (1998). This prominent computer scientist says we should "teach maintenance first . . . because in more mature subjects [than computer science] we teach reading before we teach writing."

And perhaps one more quote will be of interest here. It's one I presented earlier in Fact 44 in the context of software maintenance, but it seems quite relevant here as well.

➡ Lammers, Susan. 1986. *Programmers at Work.* Redmond, WA: Microsoft Press. Contains this quote from a then younger Bill Gates: "[T]he best way to prepare [to be a programmer] is to write programs and to study great programs that other people have written. . . . I went to the garbage cans at the Computer Science Center and I fished out the listings of their operating systems."

Conclusions

There you have it—55 facts and a few fallacies that are fundamental to the field of software engineering. You may have agreed with some of those facts and fallacies and disagreed with others. But I hope your creative juices were stimulated along the way and that your ideas for how we can do a better job of building and maintaining software have been made to flow.

Several underlying themes emerge from the facts and fallacies I've presented here.

- The *complexity* of the software process and product drives a lot of what we know and do in the field. Complexity is inevitable; we shouldn't fight it, so much as learn how to work with it. Fifteen of these facts are concerned with complexity, and a number of others are driven by it.

- Poor *estimation* and the resulting *schedule pressure* are killing us in the software field. Most runaway projects, for example, are not about poor software construction practices but about aiming for unrealistic targets. Ten facts align with this theme.

- There is a *disconnect* between software managers and technologists. This accounts for the fact, for example, that the problems that scuttle runaway projects are often known but not addressed at the beginning of the project. Five facts focus on that disconnect.

- *Hype,* and the notion of *one-size-fits-all* undermine our ability to put together project-focused, strong, sensible solutions. We continue to seek the Holy Grail while knowledgeable people tell us over and over again that we are not going to find it. Four facts are about this delusion.

There were also some underlying themes to the *sources* of these facts and fallacies. To aggregate this data, I looked at all of the sources for all of the facts and fallacies and categorized them as to whether the key players for each were academic researchers, practitioners, academic/practitioner crossovers (people who had worked in both fields), and "gurus" (my definition here is "people known for their prominently expressed opinions"). As I aggregated the data, I found myself increasingly surprised by what I found.

The dominant source for these facts and fallacies was practitioner/academics, people who had been both industry practitioners and academics during the course of their careers. People like Barry Boehm and Fred Brooks and Al Davis and myself. Roughly 60 of these sources, about 35 percent of them, came from this category. The second largest source was practitioners, people who had spent their whole career in industry. There were roughly 50, or 29 percent, of those. Academic researchers were far fewer in number than I expected—roughly 40, or 23 percent. And gurus, to my enormous surprise, were the smallest in number of all the categories, at roughly 20, or 12 percent.

I suppose this says as much about my own personal biases in selecting these facts and their sources as it does about anything else. Although I love a piece of good, evaluative academic research, I tend to be much more impressed with a piece of good, evaluative practice-grounded research. And I look at guru pronouncements with a particularly critical eye.

There are a couple of research-focused organizations that I want to single out for praise here. The Software Engineering Laboratory (SEL), a consortium of academe/practice/government, has over the years, in my opinion, been the source of the most important practice-based, academic-quality research being carried on in the software field. Kudos to NASA-Goddard (government), Computer Sciences Corp. (industry), and especially the University of Maryland Computer Science department (academe) for forming this consortium and for carrying on such important work. The software world needs more such organizations.

I would also like to cite the Software Engineering Institute (SEI) at Carnegie Mellon University for its pioneering software engineering technology transfer work. Once findings emerge from researchers, such as those at the SEL, someone must help move those research findings forward. The SEI may not always have chosen to focus on the technologies that I would have liked them to, but once they choose a technology to move forward, they do an excellent job of it.

And I would like to present here a list of people whose contributions to the facts in this book have been vital, people whose research work is solid and solidly based in reality. Kudos to Vic Basili, Barry Boehm, Fred Brooks, Al Davis, Tom

DeMarco, Michael Jackson, Capers Jones, Steve McConnell, P. J. Plauger, Jerry Weinberg, Karl Wiegers, and Ed Yourdon. Likely as not, when I spot a key finding in the software engineering world, one or more of these names will be attached to it.

Now, let me close with this. One of my favorite sayings in the software engineering world is this:

Reality is the murder of a beautiful theory by a gang of ugly facts.

I did not set out, in this book, to construct that "gang of ugly facts." Nor do I believe that every theory is necessarily beautiful. But I do believe this: Any theory worth its salt in the software engineering field is going to be consistent with the facts I have presented here, ugly or not. I would suggest that theorists whose concepts are inconsistent with one or more of these facts should think again about what they are proposing—or advocating. And I would suggest that practitioners considering some tool, technique, method, or methodology that is at odds with one or more of these facts should beware of serious pitfalls in what they are about to embark on.

Over the years, we have made a lot of mistakes in the software field. I don't mean runaway projects and failed products because I think that there are far fewer of those than many people would like us to believe. I don't mean "not-invented-here" or "it-won't-work" people because I think there are very few of those as well. The mistakes I am talking about are those that emerge from otherwise very bright people in our field who propose and advocate and install concepts that are clearly fallacious.

I hope this collection of facts and fallacies will help eliminate those kinds of mistakes.

About the Author

Robert L. Glass has meandered the halls of computing for over 45 years now, starting with a 3-year gig in the aerospace industry (at North American Aviation) in 1954–1957, which makes him one of the true pioneers of the software field.

That stay at North American extended into several other aerospace appearances (Aerojet-General Corp., 1957–1965, and the Boeing Co., 1965–1970 and 1972–1982). His role was largely that of building software tools used by applications specialists. It was an exciting time to be part of the aerospace business—those were the heady days of space exploration, after all—but it was an even headier time to be part of the computing field. Progress in both fields was rapid, and the vistas were extraterrestrial!

The primary lesson he learned during those aerospace years was that he loved the technology of software but hated being a manager. He carefully cultivated the role of technical specialist, which had two major impacts on his career:

(a) His technical knowledge remained fresh and useful, but (b) his knowledge of management—and his earning power (!)—were diminished commensurately.

When his upwards mobility had reached the inevitable technological Glass ceiling (tee-hee!), Glass took a lateral transition into academe. He taught in the software engineering graduate program at Seattle University (1982–1987) and spent a year at the (all-too-academic) Software Engineering Institute (1987–1988). (He had earlier spent a couple of years [1970-1972] working on a tools-focused research grant at the University of Washington.)

The primary lesson he learned during those academic years was that he loved having his head in the academic side of software engineering, but his heart remained in its practice. You can take the man out of industry, apparently, but you can't take the industry out of the man. With that new-found wisdom, he began to search for ways to bridge what he had long felt was the "communication chasm" between academic computing and its practice.

He found several ways of doing that. Many of his books (more than 20) and professional papers (more than 75) focus on trying to evaluate academic computing findings and on transitioning those with practical value to industry. (This is decidedly a nontrivial task and is largely responsible for the contrarian nature of his beliefs and his writings.) His lectures and seminars on software engineering focus on both theoretical and best of practice findings that are useful to practitioners. His newsletter, *The Software Practitioner,* treads those same paths. So does the (more academic) *Journal of Systems and Software,* which he edited for many years for Elsevier (he is now its Editor Emeritus). And so do the columns he writes regularly for such publications as *Communications of the ACM, IEEE Software,* and ACM SIGMIS's *DATA BASE.* Although most of his work is serious and contrarian, a fair portion of it also contains (or even consists of) computing humor.

With all of that in mind, what are his proudest moments in the computing field? The award, by Linkoping University of Sweden, of his honorary Ph.D. degree in 1995. And his being named a Fellow of the ACM professional society in 1999.

Index